Praise fo

A comprehensive and painstaking effort to document Kashmir's sacred heritage—existing, remnant, or decimated—this work should be viewed as a gut-wrenching plea for imperative and urgent remedial steps.

—**Ashwin Sanghi**, *Bestselling author*

Kashmir has been very critical to our ancient Indian civilisation, particularly for the Shaivite stream. And as all know, temples have been at the heart of our way of life. They were not just spiritual centres, but cultural and civilisations hubs, to keep the lifeblood of our ancient way flowing in a constant beat. It is no surprise therefore, that invaders repeatedly attacked our temples. The aim was not just wealth, but to wipe out that which keeps our culture alive. But history has been witness, that a civilisation does not die when it is attacked or defeated or its centres destroyed. A civilisation dies when its adherents forget. Avanti, through this book, is ensuring that we don't forget. We must remember the great temples of Kashmir, for only when we remember, can we revive. My compliments to Avanti on this very important endeavour.

—**Amish**, *Bestselling author, diplomat*

What happened to Hindu temples during 14th–20th centuries in Kashmir is the theme of book by Avanti Sopory. She describes vividly the surviving early art and architecture remains of temples. It is a must read book to know how the rich cultural heritage became victim of vandalism at the hands of intolerant fundamentalists.

—**D.P. Dubey, PhD**, *Professor*

Department of Ancient History, Culture and Archaeology
University of Allahabad

Dear Rituparna,

Hope you get to see another side of Kashmir.

Lots of love

Avanti

ANCIENT & LOST TEMPLES OF KASHMIR

AVANTI SOPORY

Readomania

Readomania
An imprint of Kurious Kind Media Private Limited
readomania.com
Email: contact@readomania.com
Facebook: facebook.com/iamreadomania
Twitter: twitter.com/iamreadomania
Instagram: iamreadomania

First Published in 2023 by Readomania

Edited by Indrani Ganguly (Managing Editor, Readomania)

Cartographer: Anil Nakhasi

The original cover picture of the Tulmul temple was gathered from the family ancestral archives. The picture was originally received from late Shri Ramji Kaul, the original resident of village Inder, Pulwama, former employee of State Electric Department, Srinagar.

ISBN: 978-93-91800-67-3

Typeset in Palatino Linotype by Shine Graphics
Printed in Delhi

For the Supreme

and

my two bundles of energy

DR. KARAN SINGH

3, NYAYA MARG,
CHANAKYAPURI
NEW DELHI - 110 021

Kashmir has been for centuries the land not only of exquisite natural beauty but an area where multiple religions and sects have flourished over the centuries. Hundreds of Hindu temples have been built down through the corridors of time. Unfortunately, most of them are in ruins and some are completely lost. There are still a very few ancient temples existing, notably the Shankaracharya, Mata Kheer Bhawani, Hairi Parbat andPandrethan. In addition, eight Bhairava temples are also in existence.

Prof. Avanti Sopory has given us a fascinating description of the lost temples of Kashmir which will evoke feeling of great sadness at the destruction of Kashmiri's magnificent temple heritage.

Karan Singh

Karan Singh
April 26, 2023

TEL. : (011) 2611-5291 2611-1744
Email : karansingh@karansingh.com

Website : www.kamakoti.org.
email : kanchimutt@gmail.com

Contact : 044-27222115
Acts : 044-27224236
Cell : 9445421115

II Sri Chandramouleeswaraya Nama: ||

Sri Sankara Bhaghavadpadacharya Paramparagatha Moolamnaya Sarvajnapeeta

His Holiness Sri Kanchi Kamakoti Peetadhipathi

JAGADGURU SRI SANKARACHARYA SWAMIGAL

Srimatam Samsthanam

No. 1, Salai Street, Kancheepuram - 631 502, Tamilnadu State, INDIA.

26th June 2023

MESSAGE OF BLESSINGS

Kashmir has been at the centre of learning, culture, philosophy, and spirituality for centuries. Much has been inspired and manifested on this land of thinkers, builders, and spiritual leaders. From Adi Shankaracharya to Abhinavagupta and from Lal Ded to Rupa Bhawani, Kashmir has been a constant source of knowledge, energy, power, and peace. Regrettably, a large part of this ancient history has been destroyed and very little is now left of it.

The book covering over 60 Ancient & Lost Temples of Kashmir, the author Avanti Kaul Sopory has attempted at giving the reader a well-researched description of many such temples which are ancient and lost. Kashmir resemble Kanchipuram of South India when it comes to temples, but ancient Kashmiri Temples are in ruins. Even the architectural remains of temple sites like Kotihar, Vijeshwara reflect on their astounding past. This book can be a guide for people who may want to visit and reconnect these ancient monuments.

Avanti herself is the great-granddaughter of Kashmir's famous Master Samsar Chand Kaul who not only was a well-known ornithologist and teacher but wrote extensively about temples, magnificent mountains, and rivers of the valley even before India's independence.

This book shall find an important place in preserving our Hindu past in Kashmir.

We are pleased to convey the Blessings of Sri Sankaracharya Swamigal of Sri Kanchi Kamakoti Peetam for this great endeavour.

For Sri Kanchi Kamakoti Peetam
Jagadguru Sri Sankaracharya Swamigal
Srimatam Samsthanam

Challa Viswanatha Sastry
Srikaryam & Agent

Map of Kashmir

Contents

Part II
Ancient Temples
(Completely decimated and lost)

Part III
Ancient Temples (Existing till date)

Part IV
The Ashtha Bhairavs

Preface

As I come back and write more about Kashmir, I must admit that this time my journey has been challenging. The first time when the idea was shared by my publisher, I agreed to it with alacrity. I did not bat an eyelid because it was about my native land. However, after hanging-up, I realized that this work will come with a huge responsibility.

Kashmir has two meanings for the larger world. There is a part of the valley which is bestowed with rivers, lakes, snowy mountains, springs, meadows, wealthy forests, primeval monuments, salubrious weather, ancient shrines, opulent gardens, and much more. And then there is the other side of the valley which is mystical, unknown, metaphysical, enigmatic, spiritual, and magical.

In the myriad centuries and generations, the above physical and spiritual aspect of Kashmir has become a quintessential characteristic of all Kashmiris. Akin to the weaving of Kashmiri carpets and shawls, every Kashmiri is a representation of the material and non-material stories that have percolated since times immemorial. There is a story in every nook and cranny of Kashmir. But no two stories are the same. A story that may sound familiar, but has a different perspective—like the moon which stays the same but people have a diverse frame of reference to it.

Ancient and lost temples are the treasured entity of the valley. Writing on the temples was challenging not because I didn't have enough information, but there were multiple sources to handle with care. Accessing, interviewing, visiting, collating, re-checking, mapping, and taking a 360-degree overview was not easy. There is no doubt that each work I have referred to, whether from ancient, medieval, pre-independence, post-independence, or modern times, has been a work of craftsmanship, kindred like the pieces of art from Kashmir.

This book reflects on the physical and spiritual past of the ancient and lost temples of Kashmir. It also attempts to showcase the architectural marvel that these temples have remained in the past. For the ease and hand-holding of the reader, this book has a unique treatment. I have introduced a fictional character Kabir, who as a research student visits these ruined temples and then collects the factual information about each temple. Kabir is the facilitator, who brings forth the fact-based truth about each of the temples he visits. I am sure the readers will enjoy this novel treatment.

The geographical location of Kashmir has always been at a strategic point. It shares borders with many countries. It was at the summit point, where the oldest and most prodigious civilizations would traverse for trade, cultural exchange, religion, war, conquest, and other such human interactions. The valley of Kashmir has remained a mature location for different religions to flourish. King Kanishka (2nd century BC) from the Kushan dynasty lent his majestic patronage to strengthen the splitting and conflicting interpretation of the basic teachings of Buddha, and because of his dynamic support and devotion, King Kanishka nurtured it throughout the length and breadth of his huge empire, of which Kashmir was a part. It is important to mention that around 70 AD, Kanishka chose Kundalavanavihara, near Harwan, about 19 km from Srinagar city, for holding the monumental religious deliberation. The Council hosted Buddhist and Hindu luminaries and produced about 3,00,000 verses on religious philosophies. Chinese traveller Hiuen Tsang has mentioned about this mega event in his writings. Under the patronage of Kanishka, Vasumitra, Asvaghosa, the council produced the commentaries known as *Vibhasha*, on Buddhist Tripitaka.

The eldest son of Guru Nanakji, Baba Sri Chand, also the founder of the Udasi sect, was once meditating next to the holy *dhuni* in Kashmir, in the 15th century. Nawab Yakub Khan, from the ruling government, accused Baba Sri Chand of instigating conflict between Hindus and Muslims. Baba immediately whacked a burning stick on the ground. No sooner he pushed the stick into the ground than the flames vanished and the stick sprouted leaves of a beautiful Chinar tree. At that moment, Baba Sri Chand said that God's tree is broad enough to give shade to everyone. What is amazing is that this Chinar tree still stands there as a monument of peace next to Shakti Sweets, at Residency Road, Srinagar city.

These exchanges led to social, physical, cultural, and religious impacts on Kashmir. Temples and shrines of Kashmir have a unique indigenous design to their structure and aesthetics. Across provinces, the temple structure broadly consisted of a garbhagriha, shikhara, mandapa, or vimana type. The other distinguishing feature was that the base of these buildings was either square or oblong, and was largely constructed out of the same material from the base to the summit. In the case of Kashmir, it was usually grey limestone. Intricate stone carvings, designs, motifs, floral patterns, and sculptures of various Gods and Goddesses are common features across Kashmiri temples.

Nags or natural water springs need special mention here. The valley abounds in glaciers, lakes, rivers, streams, and springs. There are numerous springs in the valley, and almost each spring has an associated Shiva temple in physical proximity to it, which is highly regarded by

Hindus. These springs have existed since pre-historic times in the valley and command enormous reverence from the locals.

The word 'Nags', used multiple times in the book, should not be confused with serpents. The Sanskrit meaning of *nag* is serpent or snake. But it has a different etymology in Kashmir. The aborigines of Kashmir were a group of people called the Nagas. These people were serpent worshipers and usually dwelled near a spring or water body. The *Nilamata Purana*, an ancient text dated around 6th century, which later became the base text for *Rajatarangini* written by Kalhana in the 12th century, mentions that the Nagas (aborigines of Kashmir) revered these water bodies, and the serpent deities living inside them. This brought forth the practice of *naga* worship or snake cult. The ancient text mentions that great importance was given to these *nags* (springs) by the aborigines. The four *dikpalas* (guardians of the four directions)—Bindusara in the east, Elapatra in the west, Uttaramanas in the north, and Srimadaka in the south—were Nagas.

According to Hindu cosmology, the temple is a representation of various symbols. The purpose of the temple is to serve as a superstructure, which is hence designed in such a way that right from the broad base all the lines, joints, etc. converge at one single point—a summit. These are aesthetically represented through the meru, garbha, kailasha, mandapa, etc. in the temple structure. Hence in the mystical format, the design of a temple takes the shape of a human form, which in theoretical parlance is called Vastupurusha. Starting from the lowermost moulding, which is the feet, the wings of the temple are the arms, the walls are the legs, the platform above is the shoulder and the door of the temple is the mouth. Hence, the temple is purusha and it was conceived and constructed by the means of prakriti, which is the energy represented as feminine power.

Vastupurusha is void without a resident soul. Therefore the image or the pratima of a deity gives life to Vastupurusha. This image is placed in the garbha-griha, where the atma (soul) of the temple resides. The building of temples was a sacred ritual and each building material was consecrated to God.

Besides the spiritual blessings, temples were a great venue for social and cultural events. During ancient times, temples would host melas (fairs) to celebrate festivals and auspicious days, therefore they became a great platform for all Kashmiris to interact, feast, and merry-make. According to *Nilamata Purana,* the Kashmiri society was aesthetic, liberal and free. Women enjoyed unrestricted freedom in Kashmir. Kashmiris celebrated numerous festivals, they liked singing and dancing, they visited gardens where men and women adorned one another with beautiful flowers, presented gifts to each other, played water sports, watched theatre, enjoyed the full-moon night, and listened to stories from the *Puranas*. They worshipped their Gods ardently and simultaneously pleased the demons.

Everything in Kashmir started with gratitude to the Gods. Even when the ancient city of Pravarapura (today's Srinagar) was designed by King Sri Pravarasena, in the 5th century CE, he commissioned the building of eight Bhairavnath temples at the eight entry points to the city. Bhairav is another form of Shiva that protects his devotees from fear, anger, and dreadful enemies. These eight points are still popular as the Ashtha Bhairav temples.

There is no count for the number of holy caves, springs, shrines, temples, trees, rivers, and mountains, in the valley of Kashmir. Every grain of earth is pious on this land.

Covering all these revered places in a single book would have been an unjustified endeavour. Hence, my effort in this book has been to bring out a condensed focus on temples that are not only ancient but are in oblivion. These religious places have been a testimony to the historical richness and cultural abundance of Kashmir. During my research, I came across antique and valuable texts; it is difficult to give an exact meaning to them. Therefore, I have tried to bring forth the best possible significance of these words and phrases.

My heart wrenches when I see the current state of these historical symbols of Kashmiri identity. These important shrines and religious sanctuaries were built by rulers in ancient times but unfortunately are in a dilapidated condition now. The temples mentioned don't just reflect the religious sentiments of the natives who had lived in the valley till about the 20th century, but they are a standing testimony to the architecture, dynasty, cultural depth, belief systems, understanding of customs, kingdoms, and royal descent of those times. Audacious enough, even the historic names of some of the ancient sites have been changed. Martand Temple is locally referred to as Shaitan Guffa, Haeri Parbat is also referred to as Koh-re-Maran, Anantnag is called Islamabad, Parihaspura Temples are called Kaen Shaher, to name a few. Some of the temple lands have got encroached on and sold in absentia by the ad-hoc head priest (not belonging to the valley) of the temple. The entire topography has been changed to suit the purpose of the existing majority.

Pravarsena II had built a five-domed brick temple in Srinagar city, which was next to the Zaina *Kadal* (bridge). The temple is enclosed on three sides by a stone wall and its trefoil arches are adorned with sculptured Hindu divinities. On this spot, there is a sacred spring of Kali.

This spring is in the vicinity of the Shah-i-Hamdan. The Hindu temple which was built over it by Pravarsena was called Kali-Shri. The point where it is located is still called Kalashpura, a corruption of Kali-Shri-Pur. On the wall in front of the river, the Hindus have put red ochre and worship Goddess Kali.

Across the *ghat*, near the Pathar Masjid is the shrine of Jyeshtha Bhairav and in the west of the masjid is the shrine of Vishakena Bhairav, but both are now within the limits of a graveyard.

The entire temple complex has witnessed many changes. It was converted into a graveyard and Zain-ul-Abidin's (also popular amongst Kashmiris as Bud-Shah, meaning the big king) mother's tomb is located inside.

Later, the temple was destroyed by Sultan Qutb-ud-Din (12th century Delhi Sultanate) who had built a Khanaqah (building constructed for the conglomeration of Muslim brotherhood) with that material. Even this was burnt twice but was rebuilt later.

In 1819, after the conquest of Kashmir by the Sikhs, their Governor Sardar Hari Singh ordered the demolition of the mosque citing that it was a Hindu temple. He ordered the Muslims to give up their possession. Military officer Phula Singh geared up his arms and aimed towards Pathar Masjid Ghat. Everything was ready to blow up the structure, but at the last moment, Muslims pleaded to Pandit Birbal Dhar (Kashmiri leader who was instrumental in resisting the Afghan rule with the help of Sikh rulers) and requested him to save the mosque. Pandit Birbal Dhar, with an empathetic heart, went to Sardar Hari Singh and told him that the Hindu shrine, though in the keeping of the Muslims was in the most protected condition. Destroying the mosque would only spread hatred and vengeance. Post this, Sardar Hari Singh stopped all orders of any sort of demolishment.

Rather than preserving and upkeeping the place, these treasures of the past have been left to oblivion. There are many errs that have happened and despite the degrading condition of these monuments, no official authority is taking the restoration work seriously. Different grants, commissions, and budgets were allocated but there is no concrete action on the ground yet. The agencies continue to pass the buck and play the blame game. A few that I came across during my research are listed below:

- Many structures are under no preservation or administration of any authority.
- There is no serious and focused research work on any ancient temple.
- The text on the ASI (Archaeological Survey of India) board pitched at some monuments is not clear.
- At some of the locations, the commentary given by the tour guide is grossly incorrect.
- The indispensable boundary wall at many of the monuments is missing.
- The mine of artefacts, which was ruthlessly defaced and vandalized by the invading Turks, Afghans, and Mongols, has never been restored. They still lay at the point they were hurled at by the attackers.
- The laidback attitude and lack of patronage of the ASI has had an un-bearing impact on the treasured past of Kashmir.

After the many centuries of misrule and outrageous behaviour of the Afghans, Turks, Mongols; the Hindu minority got some respite under the governance of the Dogra dynasty. It was in their rein that they brought back the dignity and confidence of the Kashmiri Hindus. It was under the Dogra rule and administration that some of the demolished and wrecked temples of Kashmir valley were restored. Dogra rulers worked tooth and nail to rebuild these temples and bring them back to their lost glory.

Their work and passion can be inspiring enough for the current team of administrators because monuments are erected for the preservation of history and cultural memory of the community. These structures are testimonials of consciousness and sensitiveness towards the distinct identity of a region.

Intent and willingness to preserve the lost legacy needs to be initiated. Although in the recent past, talks and initiations for reinstating some of the religious monuments have gained momentum, this spirit has to be maintained and well patronized. Our agencies can take inspiration from the commendable restoration work which is being undertaken at the ancient temples of Cambodia, Greece, Egypt, and many other countries, which have an astounding heritage just like India. After the seventh exodus of Kashmiri Hindus, who once were in majority in the valley; they should be at least entitled to pay obeisance to the deities, who once lived in these temples. As my great-grandfather, Master Samsar Chand Kaul wrote in his book *The Holy Spring of Kheer Bhawani*, "...The kind of close relationship that a body has with the universe, similarly Kashmir has a close relationship with the whole of India. All the pilgrimages of the Hindu religion, all deities, and all the places of pilgrimage, all of them are sub-located in one way or another in Kashmir. Kashmir's oldest historic book *Neelamt-Puraan* is the witness of this fact and it is definitely proved by public opinion..."

The oval-shaped valley of Kashmir became a favourite amongst scholars, intellectuals, researchers, and seekers of knowledge and wisdom, not only from pan-India but also the neighbouring countries. Whether it is non-dualist

Shaivism, the theory of art, Mahayana Buddhism, the enrichment of the Sanskrit language, the idea of aesthetics, the philosophy of language, the notion of erotic, the communicative role of Sharada script, Tantric rituals, works of Adi Guru Shankaracharya, the visit of Swami Vivekananda, enrichment of literary genres, writing of plays or theatre works or stories, and much more; Kashmir's contribution has been so significant in all these areas, that the history of Indian cultural tradition remains incomplete without taking them into consideration. Kashmir remains to be the fountainhead of the Indian cultural and civilizational matrix.

For the convenience of the reader, I have divided the researched temples into four prominent parts, namely:

1. The ancient temples which are in ruins but some of their remnants can be traced.
2. The ancient temples which are completely decimated and lost.
3. The ancient temples which are still existing.
4. The Ashtha Bhairavs.

Aurel Stein, in his translation of *Rajatarangini*, mentions about Kashmir, "Kashmir is a country where there is not a place as large as a grain of sesame without a Tirtha. Time and conversion to Islam of greater portion of population has changed but little in this respect. This book is therefore a humble attempt at bringing to focus the pre-historical, cultural, civilizational, religious, and intellectual enterprise and contribution of Kashmiri Pandits in the entire subcontinent."

I would like to conclude with a poem written by the famous Kashmiri poet Motilal 'Saqi', in the 1990s. The poem laments at the loss of temples, and their dismal plight.

The original Kashmiri poem is followed by the English translation.

Chhi vony mandori manz baskeen kats taam,
Vadaan vady-vady karaan tim shaam subahas,
Khabar chhakh vuny-na-vuny paeyi sheri lab paeth
Khabar chhakh asy chhi be-dasgaah, karan kyaah,
Karaan shets kaen chhu yeth mandori vusavaar,
Yi bachaeyi vaaensan ta deva doh saaeny naeran,
Achhin tal raazabal chhukh aes vaeharith.

A few dwellers still remain in the temple
They cry, their mornings turn to night
Crying.
They know any moment now,
Bricks will bury them all.
They know they are friendless,
There is nothing to be done
They console themselves:
The bricks of the old temple are still strong.
It may yet survive,
Just long enough
For us to live out our sad lives
The burning pyres stare them in the eye
With its mouth ever open.

(Poem taken from the blog 'searchkashmir')

Prologue

Kabir was anxious. Covid had delayed all his plans. He was only a few approvals away from receiving his doctorate in 'Ancient History and Architecture of Kashmir' from the University of California, but the global pandemic situation had gotten the world on its knees. International travel had been severely affected and very few flights carried full service. The University was closed indefinitely. Research students could not step out for any field study. As a result, all his research papers, field visits, questionnaires, and interviews were left sketchy and half-done. He was helpless and had no clue about his plans.

Little hope of normalcy had raised its head when his Asian neighbour had invited him for dinner that night. Nadira, a friend from Pakistan, had hosted a farewell dinner for Roshni, who had finished her course and wished to celebrate with her friends. It was an event everyone was looking forward to, especially after the many months of lull.

Nadira had set up the backyard with beautiful fairy lights and lovely diyas (earthen lamps) along the flower beds. The top of the hedge was speckled with a generous spread of bright orange marigold flowers. At the gateway, two brass urlis (decorative broad base bowls for floating diyas and flowers) were bedecked with rose petals, swaying to the tune of the summer breeze on the water's surface.

"Wow! You have been working hard on this, Nadira. Thank you. I am touched," said an excited Roshni.

"We are still so far from Eid and Diwali, yet, here, it seems like festivities are around the corner!" exclaimed Kabir.

Nadira smiled and graciously accepted the compliments. There was bonhomie all around with young men and women occupying various spots. Given the Covid situation, there weren't many people around but just enough to occupy the beautiful mirror-work floor cushions Nadira had specially ferried from Peshawar.

Kabir was happy for Roshni but it came with some other mixed feelings. His current stay in California was eating on his savings. His scholarship money was nearing its end and the online content work paid only peanuts. He hoped to earn his doctoral degree soon and secure a job as a reader at his alma mater or any prestigious university in India. But the universe had some other plans for him, which he was unaware of.

"Kabir, did you read the new circular from the HoD? He has sent an e-mail today morning," a fellow American friend checked with Kabir. Kabir had not topped up his internet data, he was late by a few days.

"I suggest you check that out. The University has written to the Embassy, and there might be a chance that students like you may get a pass for the field visit and submit your final thesis and other reports," continued the American.

Kabir couldn't wait any longer. He borrowed Nadira's laptop to log into his e-mail. There was a mail from the HoD informing students to visit the campus and restart their doctoral work. Kabir was optimistic. He stayed back post the party to help Nadira wind up, and then went back to his apartment. He dug through all the file folders and boxes hoping to align all the requisite documents, as instructed in the email.

Next, Kabir was on the flight to India. It was a long haul, sleepless hours and multiple flights from California to Srinagar, but it was worth all the wait. Amidst all the mayhem in the world due to Covid, armed with his negative RTPCR test report, Kabir did not waste a minute in reaching his destination for field study. He skipped meeting his family in Shimla and took the next connecting flight to Srinagar from New Delhi.

Shakeel, his college friend from Bangalore, had arranged his stay at his home in Ganderbal. Although Kabir wished to stay in Srinagar city and remain connected and ready for any forthcoming travel restrictions or unrest, yet he chose to stay in the picturesque town of Ganderbal.

He had a herculean task to accomplish—to visit various monumental sites and villages looking for the academic details which he had already put on the rubrics. It would not be easy. Walking through those new locations, deserted structures, sometimes hostile responses, undiscovered territories, and language, were some of the challenges for him. Although his parents spoke in Kashmiri, yet Kabir wasn't fluent in it and this could be a hindrance for him in Kashmir. It had been long since his forefathers had fled Kashmir, so citing his genealogy wouldn't help him warm up to the locals.

Incidentally, his thesis work was also a part of the last promise he had made to his bereaved grandmother—to bring to the world the rich archaeological, cultural, and religious history of the temples and monuments of Kashmir.

Part I

Ancient Temples (In ruins)

I-1
Avantiswami Temple
Pulwama

A brief visit to the Sri Pratap Singh Museum in Srinagar changed Kabir's entire itinerary. Those mutilated and excavated idols that lit brighter under the spotlight of their chambers were evidence of the great legacy they carried. Originally as per the plan, Avantisvara and Avantiswami were to be toured in the second phase of his Srinagar visit. But now it was a different story. Immediately after the visit to the museum, Kabir drove down the Anantnag road and found himself in the ancient Avantipura town.

In the ninth century, King Avantivarman founded the town of Avantipura, which was originally called Vishvaika-Sara. King Avantivarman reigned between 855–883 AD and was the founding king of the Utpala dynasty. His predecessor was King Utpalapida.

Centuries have passed since he lived on this earth but King Avantivarman is remembered as an ideal king. Under his reign, art, culture and harmony flourished in the valley. He paid attention to every minute detail, which tended to the well-being of his province and subjects. It was during his time that various engineering projects were accomplished to minimize the havoc created by floods, which was a frequent issue in the valley. He had commissioned the famous engineer Suyya for various projects and later named the now-famous town of Sopore after the great engineer Suyya.

King Avantivarman had built two magnificent temples. The first and larger one is Siva-Avantisvara and the other, a rather small but more ornate and well-preserved is the temple of Avantiswami-Vishnu. Both are built on the right side of the river Jhelum. One is in Avantipura and the other in the northwest of Jhelum, situated in the village of Jaubrar.

I-1a
Siva-Avantisvara

I-1a: Majestic steps leading to the inner sanctum.

I-1b: Triangular designed engraving on the column.

Temple Structure

The gateway to this temple is in the middle of the stone wall and is divided into two chambers by a cross wall. There are no sculptures and the niches and panels are plain. The temple is situated inside a courtyard enclosed by massive stone walls. The western side of this wall is adorned with a row of fluted columns but without any recess.

Sadly, much of the temple has been mutilated. The base of the shrine in the centre stands at an approximate height of ten inches. At each of its corners, a 16-inch square platform was attached, which originally must have supported a small subsidiary shrine. The stairs on all four sides are supported by flank walls. These stairs resemble those of Pandrethan (mentioned later in the book).

Only at one point do the platforms seem to have been attached to the plinth of the temple, afterwards they appear to be joined by a connecting wall built of architectural fragments. This arrangement is on the south-eastern corner of the base and is the only available evidence. The base of the pilaster is decorated with two seated rams and a dancing girl with a damaru standing on an ornamented throne with two lions at the sides and an elephant facing in the middle. The only existing exterior decoration of the temple base is a series of projecting facets, the largest of which was surmounted by plain rectangular capitals. Two subsidiary shrines are placed in the two rear corners of the courtyard. Kabir was disheartened to see the plight of the temple. The complex is nothing but a rumble of confused ruins. Even after exploring the place for hours, Kabir could not make much about it. The large assortment of strewn relics of a magnificent past narrated a hear-breaking story. Some of these were:

- The spandrel of an arch in front of the southern stair
- The flower and vase capital of a dodecagonal pilaster
- The spandrel of another arch by its side

I-1b
Avantiswami-Vishnu

Temple Structure

This temple was built by the aesthetic king during his youth. A colonnaded peristyle leads the way to a paved courtyard. The main shrine is built on a double base with smaller shrines on four sides. The peristyle of the temple is plain except for one side which has fluted columns. On the other three sides, there is a decoration of a rectangular string course. The pilasters on the side wall bear the figure of Vishnu and his consorts, Lakshmi and Bhumi. Vishnu possesses six arms, two of which in impartial affection encircle the bodies of his consorts; while the remaining four hold the bow, the mace, etc. Below this throne, there are two parrots and they are also on the capitals of the pilaster. The divine beings are under a canopy of an arch. A border of square rosettes, geese, flowers, and lion heads accentuates the panel.

The God and Goddesses on the opposite pilaster are more ornamented. While the Gods have four arms here, the Goddesses are adorned with two arms only. Neatly brushed hair, roses inserted in the braids, intricately designed jewellery, necklaces, and a *mandaramala* (garland of celestial flowers) emphasize the appearance of the Gods. The Goddesses' beauty is highlighted by exaggerated breasts, slim waits, and hanging earlobes (suggesting the heavy weight of the earnings) and three-tier tiaras.

The entrance to the shrine is after a flight of a few steps and opens on the west wall. The 69 cellular colonnade is the prized beauty of the temple. All of them are preceded by 24-sided columns on plain square bases.

A string of ten dhoti-clad men and women is sculptured on the inner surface of the southern pilaster. All of them are in a spirit of devotion to Vishnu. On the opposite pilaster, there is a similar group of ten figures, consisting of a bearded and crowned male and a lady who is seen wearing a scarf that hangs down on her shoulder. There is another pair of a male and female, who seem to be the attendants.

The wall surfaces, both internally and externally, are exhaustively sculptured with large female figures of Ganga and Yamuna, seated on crocodiles and tortoises respectively. On the right-hand pilaster of the wall, there is an ornamented figure of a king and his two queens seated on a *simhaśana* (lion throne). On the two external sides of this pilaster, the lions have been replaced by two standing females—in the southern panel the king is standing in *abhaya* (fearless) posture, and a lady is looking into a round-pocket mirror and admiring her charm. In the other two panels, the figures are seated on separate cushions but share the same long cushion.

The walls and the rectangular panels have carvings of animals, and figures of males and females. They consist of decked-up elephants who are fighting with horned birds of monstrous size, a male and two female *chauri* (flywhisk made of the yak's tail) bearers, of men standing with folded hands between two human-headed birds with a row of *kirtimukhas* adorning the top, of Garuda engraved in circular panels, of a male and two females seated in a joyous mood, of cups of wine, of doves cooing and billing around, of Goddess Ganga, of four-armed Atlas wearing a cushion-like head dress, of pairs of male and female figures standing on the narrow facets of the niche. These are the only remnants of the magnificent piece of art that was created here centuries ago. There are ruins all around the complex, yet the rumble is so beautiful. The sidewalls of the flight of steps are covered with sculptured relief and each of the smaller panels is facing the courtyard depicting erotic scenes.

Between the main shrine and the gateway, there is a stepped stone. It must have been the place for the Garudvaja. Garuda is the divine vehicle of Vishnu and also shown as an emblem on Vishnu's flag. The sanctum has disappeared but only the base and a few stones on the north wall are intact.

There are five shrines in the courtyard. The decorative temples dedicated to the panchratnas (sapphire, diamond, ruby, pearl, coral—the five jewels), are arranged in a quincunx. In the northeast, a spout at the pedestal has been carved in the shape of a *makara* (crocodile), indicating that this shrine was dedicated to Goddess Ganga. In the north, a water trough indicates that this water was used for washing the deity inside the sanctum.

Material used

The temple is built out of massive and solid stones. The mobility of these grey granite stones is beyond normal human strength. The boulders are interlocked and carved with artistic fineness.

What caused the downfall

The temple has witnessed a lot of destruction even during Hindu rule. King Kalasa (1081–1089 AD) seized the temple and forced the villages to be under his reign.

After the accession of King Jayasimha (1128 AD) to the royal throne, Bhasa, a commander of the existing royal troops was held captive inside the Avantiswami temple by Damaras of the Holada (Wular) district.

Many new-generation locals say that a massive earthquake shook the temple and ruined the complex completely. There is another group of natives who claim that a devastating flood swept away the temple complex and left behind the ruins.

Historians claim that in the 14th century, Sikandar Butshikan destroyed the temple.

Current state

A 20 feet deep pit is where the temple stands now. Amongst the small houses, lofty mountains, golden fields, and orchards stands this mammoth mystery of so many broken pieces. The mammoth structure has crumbled now, but still holds the story of a splendid past. Willow or poplar trees and a thick orchard girdle the dilapidated temple premise.

On either side of it, one can still see the precarious remains of the massive columns supporting a portico.

A huge collection of antiques was excavated from the temple site and is now displayed at Sri Pratap Singh Museum in Srinagar. These include large jars and containers, which may have been used for keeping food items and dry rations. Some have been found to have the inscription of King Avantivarman.

What next

Like most other monuments, this set of temples is crying for restoration and promotion. The road to the temple should be well accessible. For most passers-by, this temple is a blink-and-miss structure. The signboards should be bigger and pitched at a more prominent crossing.

Also, most importantly, the local guides have to be well educated and trained on the information shared with the tourists. There should be a check on quack guides, who sometimes misinform the tourists. The tourism ministry should have pre-designed literature or a pamphlet that the tourist can refer to.

This can be a beautiful venue for any cultural event or any such seminar. The authorities can look at such possibilities too.

I-2

Bumzu Cave Temple

Anantnag

Kabir's grandmother had once mentioned about the district of Anantnag to him. She hadn't been there ever but desired to set feet at the land of her ancestors. She wasn't alive to live the dream, but for Kabir, this was a compelling reason to visit Anantnag. While he was researching on Anantnag, he understood that it was called by different names like 'The granary of Kashmir' or 'Gateway to Kashmir Valley'. It got its name from the *anant* (many) *nags* (springs) that originated from the southern side of the town. This has been corroborated through Kalhana's *Rajatarangini, Valley of Kashmir* by Sir A. Stein and various historians of the valley. Even the *Nilamata Purana* mentions the spring as a holy place for the Hindus.

Kabir had a few notes about the Bumzu Cave Temple scribbled in his old diary. Through those notes, he remembered that there were many small temples in the district. The largest amongst them was identified as the Bhimakesava shrine, which was built by Queen Didda's maternal grandfather, King Bhima Shahi of Gandhara. Kabir was aware that Queen Didda ruled as regnant-queen over Kashmir between 980–1003 AD. She was called the 'Witch Queen', by the locals. In modern times, she was referred to as the 'The Catherine of Kashmir'.

Bumzu is only a mile to the north of the sacred springs of Mattan and contains the only remaining group of artificial caves in Kashmir.

Temple Structure

There are three temple caves situated on the left bank of the Lidder river. Of all three, only one possesses architectural interest. It is located on a raised platform and can be reached through a flight of stairs. It is carved out of a large chunk of a limestone cliff. Since the stone is friable in nature, therefore the façade of the gateway has been built in stone masonry in lime.

I-2a: Trefoil façade designed in the hillock.

This cliff overlooks the entire Lidder Valley. There is no record or tradition as to the time of the construction of the temple. But from the simple and rudimentary style of the temple's construction, historians suggest that it must have been built around the 1st or the 2nd century.

The gateway consists of a trefoil-arched doorway, surmounted by a pediment and the side walls. The left side wall has a small, rectangular niche measuring approximately two and a half square feet. Floral scrolls of extraordinary delicacy have been carved out on the pilasters. The lintel is decorated with a remarkable row of rosettes and the cornice with a row of slightly projecting dentils. It is a wonder to notice how the intervening spaces have been filled with the figures of dancing dwarfs, which unfortunately have been defaced now. The temple in the interior is 81 square feet and stands on a base of 4 feet 6 inches in height. There is a slight projection of the porch, which points to it being decadent. The corner pilasters have two rectangular niches.

A huge stone carved out like a cuboid has a hole pitched in the middle. It is assumed that the main deity was placed here or it was used for pitching the royal flag.

Once inside, there are two raised platforms on the left side and right side of the cave respectively. While the right side is blank, the left side has two Shiva-lingas. A big and a small one. They both are only a few steps away from each other. While the small Shiva-linga has an arrangement for the water to be drained out, the big Shiva-linga does not have any such arrangement. It is dark inside with no sliver of light, other than just the main door. The floor surface is uneven and there are many big and small platforms and steps that have been laid out. Around the simple cella, there is a narrow track for the circumambulation of the main God.

The inner roof of the cave is jagged and uneven. The hues of the rocks are discoloured. Some stone carvings on tiles have a rough and shabby sculpturing. They are placed next to the wall. Researchers believe that they must have been part of the initial plan, but were not then used during the building of the temple.

At the foot of the cave, there are two temples, but over time, they have been converted into Muslim ziarats (shrines). Both are under a thick coat of mud plaster. It is believed that under this blanket many artistic and archaeological features are concealed. Between the two temples, the larger one is popular by the name of Ziarat of Baba Bamdin Sahib, who was said to be a disciple of Sheikh Nur-ud-din, the famous Nund Rishi.

The pyramidal roof is buried under a heap of mud which surmounts the modern square double wooden roof. But the entrance to the temple is from the north. Unless the plaster is cleared, it is difficult to say if the temple has an opening from the other side too. Here the interior measures 64 square feet. The overlapping stones on the ceiling are similar in look to the Pandrethan temple (mentioned later in the book). The uppermost stone is carved with blossomed lotus. The ruins of the smaller temple can be seen to the west of this temple. There is nothing clear and visible on the exterior of the roof. It has all been destroyed. Interestingly, the ceiling inside is intact and is similar to the ceiling of the large temple. The porches are an exact replica of the cave temple. Historians infer that all three temples may have been built around the same time.

I-2b: Inner arched cella.

The small alcoves on the left and right side of the outer wall are vacant and there are no signs of anything ever placed there.

Material used

Limestone is the common construction material used inside. The façade of the temple is carved out of the hillock.

What caused the downfall

Unlike other temples in Kashmir, this one did not face any destruction or mutilation of any kind. Perhaps that's because it was inside a cave and was not prominent like the other temples, which displayed a *shikhar* or a flag.

But this temple has witnessed the vagaries of time and over the many centuries has remained a still witness to the changing social and demographic fabric of Kashmir.

Current state

The stairs going up to the cave are in their original state. The old square doorways are defaced now.

The steps to the stairs are steep and are constructed out of huge slabs of limestone. The small cella inside stays uninterrupted. The two Shiva-lingas inside are at their original place, but the imprints of modern times are visible on them. Many village houses have mushroomed around the sides.

In the vicinity, there is a touch of urbanization. ASI has put up an information board, and a bench for resting at a platform between the long flight of stairs. This platform is ancient and was there from the beginning.

What next

The first thing that catches the attention of the visitor is the audacious attempt at concealing the word 'India' from the signage of 'Archaeological Survey of India' on the information board. This comes across as scornful, especially when the information board itself says that any attempt to deface, alter, etc. at any official property shall be dealt with seriously.

There is serious work to be done towards spreading information about the distinct monumental history of Kashmir. The State and Central authorities have a responsibility at preserving these sites. Creating events, printing brochures, training guides, creating a list of 'must-visit' sites in Kashmir can help in bringing back the lost glory of the valley. There is a lot of scope for social scientists from across the world to conduct their research and bring out papers on these monuments.

Kabir's closing note in his diary were stories and anecdotes that he had collected from locals living around the temple. Legend says that around 993 BC, Raja Nara succeeded his father Vibhishana. During his reign, the beautiful daughter of Naga King Susravasa, named Chandrasaha, was married to a simple Brahman and lived by a lake near Vitasta. One day, Raja Nara was visiting the lake and was besotted by Chandrasaha. He admired how gracefully she moved through the calm waters. At length he planned to take her away from the Brahman. As would be, the Brahman approached King Susravasa and they all ensured that King Nara's plan failed. A storm was called upon, the earth opened up. King Nara along with his entire court was swallowed up by the earth. In retaliation, the serpent king's sister hurled a big stone from the Bawan Mountains at the city. The caves of Bumzu are said to be on the spot where these rocks were upturned.

I-3
Buniar Temple
Baramulla

The internet was patchy and frustrating. Kabir moved from one room to the other trying to catch the data signal. All he wished was to Google whether Bhavaniyar, Bhaniyar, Bunair, Buniyar, Boniar, Buniar, Boniyar were the different names for the same Buniar temple that he had come researching for.

He waited for some time but Google wasn't of much help, so he decided to visit the location personally. He had no clear coordinates for the temple complex but Shakeel's family guided him with the location. He boarded the Baramulla bus and dismounted at the bus stop next to the roaring Jhelum.

Buniar temple, which many describe as the 'best preserved' specimen of Kashmiri temple architecture, is next to a military camp. It is called by different names, depending on the local dialect and the vernacular way of pronouncing the name.

While strolling around, Kabir overheard a local villager saying that during the late 19th century a *fakeer* was the caretaker of the temple. This *fakeer* had asserted that only a giant race could accomplish building a giant temple like Buniar.

Temple Structure

The gateway is a double-chambered structure facing a trefoil arch. The interior consists of a lofty central edifice,

I-3a: Fluted pillars with intervening trefoil-headed recess.

which is located in a large quadrangle and is surrounded by a colonnade of fluted pillars with intervening trefoil-headed recesses. Over time these flutes have worn off and are not conspicuous. The exterior of the walls is surmounted by a cornice of *kirtimukhas.*

The ground floor is square in shape with pilasters at the corners. These pilasters are 4 feet in thickness. The interior is a square of about 13 feet thick and the walls are about 6 feet thick. This sturdiness of the building is a sound proof of the antiquity of the temple.

On the western and eastern sides, a flight of steps give way to the entry and exit of the temple. The flight of steps on the roadside is buried underground. The inner staircase consists of seven steps flanked by sloping rails. There is a small stone platform placed between the temple and the stairs. This is the lowest course of the stepped base of a Garudadvaja column.

Access to the sanctum is through a lofty trefoil arch which stands upon an advanced pilaster. An enclosed rectangular entrance originally surmounted by an ornamental trefoil and steep pediment adds beauty to the entrance of the temple. Jambs of the entrance are adorned with half-engaged columns. Like most ancient temples, this one too stands on a double base.

Inside the main temple, the pedestal of the image which originally must have been of Vishnu is placed on a broad platform. Over time, this has been replaced by many small Shiva-lingas, originally procured from the bed of river Narmada. In 1865, when Bishop Cowie visited the temple complex, he described the ceiling spring as dominical. Over time this ceiling either fell or was removed. The stone used in the construction of the ceiling was known as Kanait, which was similar to Kanjur of Taxila. There are pieces of evidence of Sharada inscription of Ramadeva on the stone structures.

The only decoration one can see on the exterior are the trefoils of the recesses, their pediments, the cornice of *kirtimukhas* and the miniature trefoils from which the roof sprang.

The campus has 53 cells along with the gateway, which is 7 feet tall and 4 feet wide. Each cell has a trefoil entrance enclosed in a high-pitched pediment resting on a half-engaged column. These cells stand on a base similar to that of the temple. A transverse beam connects the capitals of the columns with the roof of the cells. The top of the cell is decorated with frieze, like the beams of the cells.

A spout of the channel which carried the washing of the image was projected from the cornice. This stream of water seemed to be in the shape of a *makara,* and right below it is a huge water trough carved out of a single block of stone. The rainwater in the courtyard is carried off by a drain which runs under the south-eastern corner of the peristyle.

Beginning from the corner of the nearest gateway is cell number 11. A side entrance near this cell continues to be closed by a wooden door. Immediately outside this side door is a square structure made of stone. Archaeologists haven't been able to find out the reasons for this structure. Much of the centre stones of the walls have come off. The external face of the western wall is partially relieved by rows of small square projections. In its corners are two cells which are opening towards the outside.

This temple is considered to be the best example of a Vaastu-compliant building in entire Kashmir. General A. Cunningham, a British archaeologist and historian, is of the opinion that the temple Bhaniyar or Bhwaniyar was dedicated to the Goddess Bhawani, the wife of Shiva.

I-3b: Cells with trefoil entrance in the compound.

Material used

The structure is built out of pale coarse granite and at some places kanait stone has been used. It is the only temple built of granite stone with a whitish colour. The granite stones have been ferried from far away because there are no granite quarries in the vicinity of the Jhelum river. The might and will of the labourers and the craftsmen who would have ferried and sculptured these beautiful pieces is remarkable. One can only imagine the exceptional strength that these extraordinary human beings possessed.

Current state

Research says that the original statue of the 5th century was vandalized and many years later a stele was placed for worship. The same stele with a very crude workmanship continues to be there and has been smeared with a bright vermillion paste. Another similar stele, still kept in the same position as it was found out, is seen lying in front of the temple stair.

Despite being located inside a thick foliage of trees, the temple was visited by many British and foreign researchers. They concluded that since the temple was so well covered by a blanket of tall trees, the nasty invaders were unable to lay their hands on it.

In 1835, Austrian explorer Karl Alexander Hügel declared it to be a Buddhist temple and in 1837 British traveller G.T. Vigne said it was a Hindu temple ruin. They were amongst the early explorers of the place. Again in 1847, explorer Alexander Cunnigham derived that the temple got its name from 'Bhawani', another name for Goddess Durga. In 1868, when archaeologist Henry Hardy Cole and photographer John Burke arrived at the temple complex to research for their 'Archaeological Survey of India Report—Illustrations of Ancient Buildings in Kashmir', they were informed by a native that the temple was built by the Pandavas from the *Mahabharat*. Despite all the hardships of the acute wintertime, these explorers were able to click some early pictures of the temple. James Fergusson, a Scottish architectural historian had also visited the temple in 1876, and he shared his architectural feedback on the complex in his works.

Although the temple dates back to the 5th or 6th century, there is yet no clarity on who commissioned the temple. Some native Pandits say that the temple was built by a person called Bonadutta and the temple is called Boniyar after him. Historian Sir A. Cunningham was of the opinion that the name of the temple implies that it was dedicated to Goddess Bhawani.

What next

The temple site is in need of urgent attention from the state authorities and ASI. Maybe the temple is not as damaged as the rest of the temples of the valley, but the cracks caused by nature and time on the structure require maintenance and reclamation. A brief informational brochure or a leaflet about the history of the monument can come handy for any visitor. Promoting the place not only as a historical venue but even as a event destination for the locals of Baramulla and Uri can project the site on a state and national level.

I-4
Bandi Temple
Baramulla

Kabir wasn't sure of his prior knowledge about this temple site. Was this temple called Bandi or Dhattamandir? He had researched and scanned all books and papers. He had even called up relatives and distant referrals in search of the truth. But all in vain. Restless and eager, he hopped into the car and put Baramulla on the map. The map showed the temple at a distance of 22 km from Baramulla on the Baramulla–Uri road.

Temple Structure

I-4a: Main temple structure along with subsidiary shrine in the front corner.

The temple which dates back to the 9th century is one of the most ancient temples in the valley. The ground plan of the temple is built on an area of 23 square feet.

This temple does not possess any colonnade. Amongst the porches, three contain closed doorways. These porches are 16 feet tall and approximately 2 feet wide. The doorways have square tops with straight mouldings and are surmounted by pediments containing trefoil ornaments. A flight of steps takes the visitor to the womb of the shrine, but inside the colonnade is entirely missing.

The jambs of the cell were decorated with half-engaged columns. These adorations on the jambs can still be seen in the southwestern corner of the peristyle.

The central shrine is built out of beautiful green limestone and faces the northeast direction. Over time, this green limestone has been covered with a thick coat of lime plaster. The wall of the structure still has some layers of coat clinging to its face. Two replicas of the main building can be seen in the northwest corner of the courtyard.

The bases of the columns which had supported the trefoil arch of the gateway are still in use. Fragments of columns as well as their beautiful carved capitals are lying about in the compound and some are outside the gateway.

A few yards to the southeast of the temple are the remains of two similar shrines which like the subsidiary temples are in the courtyard. They are the replicas of the main temple. The construction of this intricately detailed temple is extremely good and is well preserved. A few carved capitals and two bases of the columns on either side of the porch are pleasing and well-detailed.

There are two platforms reached by five steps situated to the right of the main porch on the ground, which is paved with stones and which was a water tank. The way to the temple must have been over a stone causeway of which only the central prier is extant. An image of Lord Hanuman is carved out of the green stone. Some experts say that it was a Buddhist monument while others assert that it was a Hindu temple dedicated to Goddess Kali.

There are many legends about this temple. Some say that it was built by the Pandavas during their exile. Bheem, who was the strongest among the five brothers, had ferried the huge boulders from the nearby mountains to construct the temple. It was dedicated to Lord Vishnu. 'Bheem Ka Matka' is another fascinating point of interest in the premise of the temple. This pot is as deep as 5 feet under the earth. It is believed that Bheem used to fill water from the nearby Vitasta river for his four brothers and Draupadi into this pot. The extraordinary legend is that irrespective of the amount of water taken out from the pot, it never ran dry.

I-4b: Carved niche on the front part of the gateway.

Material used

Unlike most temples which are built out of granite, this temple is constructed out of rough kankar stone. Only the plinth is made out of limestone. There is also a lot of use of green limestone.

What caused the downfall

The temple has been left in oblivion for a long time. There hasn't been much information that historians could trace or reveal about the reasons for this temple's deterioration. Certain studies say that a lot of damage was done to the temple during the 1947 raider attack from across the border. Like many other magnificent temples of Kashmir, even this one was desecrated and destroyed. The ancient idols, sculptures, and motifs were shattered and knocked down multiple times.

Current state

The temple comes under the maintenance of ASI and locally it is under the maintenance of the Army. The main entrance door jhamb is painted bright yellow. The sanctum inside has a few pictures of Gods and Goddesses. The Army has installed a Shiva-linga on the premises and they guard the complex. Small residential houses can be spotted outside the temple boundary.

The ASI brief on the bulletin board about the temple is the only sign of information that is available. A handful of people living near the temple complex have formed a group and look after the temple in turns. However, there aren't many visitors.

What next

There is a lot that can be done to bring the site up to the mark. Other than restoring the temple which is most important, the local guides need to be given correct information about the temple. Any misleading data can do more harm than good. Probably a pre-designed informative script can be shared as a brochure about the temple.

I-5
Fatehgarh Temple
Baramulla

It had been almost a month since Kabir had been out and about in the valley. He wanted a break from his research work and accepted a lunch invite from a friend in Baramulla. He drove the one-and-a-half hours distance alone. It was a broad road with a vista of willow trees on both sides of the road.

Nearly 3 miles away from Baramulla, something attracted his attention. He spotted the ruins of a very large temple. These ruins are located at the mouth of the beautiful Narwav Valley. A notice by ASI prepared Kabir for a more majestic temple of Shiva and his consort. It read, 'You are within the 100-metre prohibited zone limit of this protected monument.'

Temple Structure

I-5: Main temple structure.

At Fatehgarh village stood the ruins of a temple which were about two-thirds of its height above the earth's surface. The compound of the temple is 47 square feet. Internally, it is approximately 850 square feet. A large part of the cella had a massive platform on which sat the colossal Shiva-linga. A large fragment of the linga lies down on the ground. It is carved out of brownstone and has some carvings on the two sides. On one side is the carving of Shiva with three heads and on the other side, a figure representing the Bhairava form of Shiva.

This platform was beautified with torus moulding and the space around this was used for *pradikshn*. There must have been a *pranali* or a water spout, which now lies on the ground of the sanctum. Two trefoil niches decorate the front of the platform. This, archaeologists assumed, must have been a place to keep the evening lamps, usually lit in the temple premise at dusk.

The doorway faces the northwest. The other three sides of the temple are covered by a large trefoil arch surmounted by a pediment. This pattern is also found in the Bunair temple. The pilaster is adorned with half-engaged fluted columns.

One of the most remarkable features of the Fatehgarh temple is the elaborate system of corbelling. Unlike other temples, where the stones are overlapped which gradually lessens the span, this temple has a distinct style of stone arrangement.

During one of the recent excavations of the temple, a few steles were discovered. They weren't great in their artistic skill but the lower one displayed human figures seated on a stool kind of a thing and the upper one displayed a trident. A row of pediment niches adorns the dado of the portico.

The temple dates back to the 8th century but there is no clarity on the name of the king who got the temple built. There was political instability during the 8th and 9th centuries. Post the fall of King Sankaravarman, his successors were not able to sustain their reign for a long time. As a result, frequent change in rulers was inevitable.

During the reign of Maharaja Ranjit Singh, a fort was built around the temple, and the stones of its pyramidal roof were used for the construction of the walls of defence. Since then the boundary walls look the same.

Material used

The entire temple is carved out of brown, grey and black coloured limestone. The stone sizes are huge and one wonders which mammoth animal or human figures would have ferried these and placed one on top of another. The black limestone is as big as 11 feet in length, 4 feet in height and 3 feet in thickness. It is a piece of wonder for anyone who would look at the temple. The general construction, the façade, the architecture and everything about the temple is magnificent and reflects the glorious past and strength of the king who would have commissioned the temple.

Current state

A thriving village around the temple complex permits only a portion of the temple to be visible. Much like the Parihaspura temple, there are piles of huge stones lying all around the complex. The Shiva-linga, which once adorned the sanctum, is now left unattended in one corner of the compound. Swarms of bees have built their colonies in the chasm and gaps of the huge complex. With no visitors of faith, the temple is only a relic from the glorious past. For the locals, it is undoubtedly a place of awe. They visit the place to experience the grandeur and risk walking on top of the wall.

A mound laden with beautiful green grass has a Chinar tree growing at the top. The tree gives a beautiful backdrop to the temple complex. It is yet to be discovered if the Chinar tree was always there or if it was sowed many years after the temple was constructed.

What next

The temple complex comes under the maintenance of ASI, Government of India. Due to neglect and perils of time, the temple has become a site of abandoned and disarrayed boulders. There is a lot that can be done here.

Events for promoting the architectural treasure of the place, hosting and organizing discourses on the ancient history of the temple and focussed preservation of the site by the authorities are some of the small steps which the authorities can take up. Without changing the structure and glory of the temple, the site can be restored and revamped into a 'must-visit' place in Kashmir.

Kabir left the complex with mixed feelings. *The air is thick with the smell of you, a labour of devotion, by whom?*

I-6

Kothair Temple

Anantnag

Mutsakund razas manshihandi kan
Tim kati baliyas? Kothair van.

(King Mutsakund had buffalo ears: where will they be removed? In the woods of Kothair.)

This is a popular adage that still goes around. During King Ananta's time (1025–63 AD), a tank was constructed by the Raja of Deccan named Matshakund. Legend has it that his ears were the size of a buffalo and he tried all possible ways to get rid of these ears. Once during his travels he was near the Kapteshwar *tirtha* (near the Kothair village), and at that time to his astonishment he spotted a wounded dog that had got healed after taking a dip in the *nag*. Raja Matshakund immediately took a dip in the 'Papshodan *nag*' (sin washer in Sanskrit), and got rid of his disfigured ears.

Approximately 10 km away from Verinag in the Arpath Valley there is a village called Kothair. In this village is the famous spring and temple called Papshodan *nag*. This temple spring finds a mention in *Rajatarangini*, but with a different name—'Kapteshwara *Tirtha*'. Even Kalhana mentions in his historic book, that if you have committed any sins, then come to this *nag tirtha*, take a dip and wash them off.

This temple invites many legends. Another one recorded by Kalhana says that a man named Padmaraja, an importer of tambala leaf, became friends with King Bhoja of Malwa. The king offered gold for the construction of a pool at Kapatesvara and vowed to wash his face daily with the water of the spring. As a mark of respect, Padmaraja would arrange to send a large glass filled with holy water from the *tirtha* for the king.

Nilamata Purana and Jaydratha in *Haracaritacintamani* have mentioned Shiva's appearance as a sandalwood piece floating on the spring. The canto described in *Haracaritacintamani* has now become the official mahamaya of the Kothair *tirtha*.

Shakeel had accompanied Kabir on his visit to Kothair temple, but he had to abruptly leave for some urgent University work. He had slipped in an envelope in Kabir's diary with all information he could gather about Kothair temple. Shakeel had sourced all this from his friends and families based at Anantnag, which is the closest town to Kothair.

I-6: Circular water body or *nag*.

Temple Structure

The temple is built in a huge area. One can see a huge tank of water, which is sourced from a natural spring. Then around the circular water body is a dismantled structure of buildings and temples. The circular tank is approximately 55 metres in diameter. The depth of the tank is considerable and a solid wall around can still be seen. Steps that lead down to the tank are seen at one end of the *nag*.

To the north of the spring is the structure of a temple. King Matsukand is ascribed to the creation of this temple. It is built in the typical Kashmiri style of architecture. There are still smaller cellars around the complex. They are constructed in a row and appear to be the lodging of the priests presiding over the deity. The pillars have been carved but they are roughed out on the edge and have missed their fineness over time.

Towards the south of the spring are a few other structures. They are independent cellas, of which one is razed and the other is a hollow cella. This one has a mandala engraved on the roof but the Shiva-linga and the Nandi are missing. Two temples seem to be contemporaneous with the stone wall of the spring.

The large temple measures eight feet four inches internally and faces southwest. Its roof seems to have been destroyed by fire. The entrance is three feet and eight inches by six feet. The recess on the outer wall of the other three sides is much smaller in this case. This is in contrast with the many other temples of the valley.

The smaller temple faces the west and measures six feet and four inches internally. The lower part of the temple is buried underground. On the northern side, there is a long stretch of wall, which is 246 feet long and about 12 feet wide and was originally part of the enclosure wall around the temple and the tank. The top stones of the cell are visible. The fragment on the eastern side, which is above ground shows that this surrounding wall is in reality a cellular peristyle.

The stone basin of the tank, built by King Bhoja, is still partially extant. The flights of steps flanked by side walls are surmounted by the cornices, which is usually seen in most Kashmiri temples, are facing north and south respectively.

Upon excavation of areas around the tank, several shrines belonging to the 10th and 11th centuries were exhumed. A cellular quadrangle was also unearthed. Stratigraphic evidences reveal that these shrines were superimposed over an older stratum of buildings.

Another curious lore suggests that treasure lies buried under the mounds and earth in and around the spring. It further says that the path and the exact location of these treasure reservoirs are inscribed on the stone slabs which are embedded in the wall of the spring. These stone slabs even have the details on expenditure on the repair and upkeep of the spring and its dependant shrines.

Material used

The relics depict that the temples were built of sand and graphite stones. Like most other temples of Kashmir, these stones are found commonly in the valley.

What caused the downfall

There has been no recorded account of what led to the downfall of the structure. Unfortunately, most ancient text and information about the temples, scriptures, spiritual and philosophical text of Kashmir has mercilessly been destroyed by the invading Islamic conquerors. As a result, the history to most of the tressured past is unavailable.

The entire complex is in an extremely pitiable state and is used as a public park with no measures to safeguard the monument.

Current state

Unlike the other destroyed temple complexes of Kashmir, where the heap of stones is stationed in one place, at Kothair van, the expanse of the complex is so large, that there is a pile of a damaged structure at every possible corner.

The barriers put around the circular spring are the only display of maintenance, while the rest of the place is in shambles. Extreme negligence by the ASI and the other concerned authorities has left the temple complex in a pitiable state.

Even a non-analyst can read the misery of the mounds, which are hiding millions of stories underneath them.

What next

The first thing that needs attention is to put up a decent signage about the site. Along with that a brief history and the name of the king who commissioned the construction of the temple should be displayed.

Temple name tags should be put outside each temple cell. The temple site needs to be listed on the tourist map of Kashmir. The place has immense potential for researchers, tourists, historians, etc. The complete complex should be protected by a boundary wall.

"Did you get to see the sandalwood log?" asked Shakeel over a phone call.

Kabir chuckled at the question and said, "Now what has that got to do with the temple?" There were so many legends he had heard during his visit to the Kothair temple, that he had lost count of them.

"Well, my grand aunt who lives in Anantnag, had told me that Shiva is believed to appear in the disguise of a sandalwood log floating on the water. So did you see anything?" enquired Shakeel. "She even said that a Brahmin named Graparasar stood in great penance and even went on to decay his body because he wanted Shiva to appear to all human beings. At that moment the lord of the lords, Shiva promised to appear in the form of a wooden log of sandalwood along with Nandi," added Shakeel.

"Yeah, I spotted some *pann-vather* (golden sun-dried Chinar leaves) floating on the top," Kabir replied. Kabir thought to himself that he should probably take a dip in the Papshodan *nag* first to wash off his sins and then hope to find the sandalwood log in the *nag*.

For Kabir, visit to each new temple became more mystical and metaphysical than the previous one. Eager to get back on his laptop, he researched further and found out that Abu-i-Fazal in his book *Ain-i-Akbari,* has mentioned that when the water in the spring decreases, an image of Shiva in sandalwood appears. Shiva manifests annually in the form of a floating piece of wood on the spring. Further, even in *Ain-i-Akbari,* Abu-i-Fazal has mentioned, "In the village of Kothair is a deep spring which when evacuated of all the water, shows an image of Mahadev in sandalwood."

I-7

Logripora Temple

Anantnag

One kilometre away from the shrine of Ashimukqam is the abode of Shiva-Shakti. Logripora is an ancient village in the assembly of Pahalgam. It has the distinction of being the holy place where both Shiva and Shakti are worshipped. This place has an ancient black monolithic *shila,* dating to the Satisar times. Hence, it is also popular by the name of Ragnya temple, after Goddess Ragnya, who is a greatly revered Goddess among Kashmiri Pandits.

The surrounding areas consist of Sapt-rishi springs in the east, Bodhi-rishi, the seat of Bodhisattva in the south, Roz-Mubarakk of Saint Zain Shah at Ashimukqam in the north and the sweet water spring in the village of Manzgam in the west.

Temple Structure

The temple complex is located amongst a cluster of Chinar and Deodar trees. It has many small units of temples inside. On the top of a small hillock is the holy spring. It is square in shape and there is a small

I-7a: Shiva-linga lying under a Chinar tree in the compound.

place for devotees to sit and worship. It is spread over an area of 40 canals.

Upon coming downhill, there is a small temple with an alcove designed in the wall. The place is empty and there is no picture or any form of representation of the Goddess there. But originally this was the place where the black monolith *shila* was placed in the sanctum. According to locals, there are many narratives to this. Some believe that the original *shila* was placed by Lord Hanuman, who had got it from Sri Lanka, en route to Mata Kheer Bhawani at Tulmul. They further add that this original monolithic stone was destroyed and taken away by either looters or antique smugglers. Their carved-out place is empty and can be approached only from over the spring, which is in the centre of the cella.

As one walks around, there are many small structures which are broken, destroyed, and vandalized. A wooden carved door, with some text inscribed in Sharada script, leads to a sort of common or assembly hall. In the vicinity is the *yagna* room. A room where the *shlokas* from the holy scriptures must have reverberated during the offerings to Shiva-Shakti. It has a fireplace in the centre, which hasn't been lit in ages.

The five springs in the temple complex have separate sources and represent the five elements of life. Later, these springs join to form a brook. These springs and the aligned temples date back to Rishi Kashyap's time. In colour, they have a black tinge and hence are called *Kali nag*.

A small structure which houses a Shiva-linga is built with simple bricks. Here the *yoni* is built in a square shape, which was a prevalent style during those times.

The base of the Shiva-linga is on a hard black monolithic stone. This one seems to have been untouched by anyone. Perhaps the stone was heavy for the invaders to lift or maybe they missed noticing it in the thick foliage of the area.

In the temple premises, there are plenty of mutilated ancient pieces, probably razed from the temple or left mid-way by the looters. Amongst them is another stone Shiva-linga, which is laying still next to the trunk of a Chinar tree. Alongside are small tiles and half-vandalized idols.

Material used

The temple is carved out of bricks, stones, wood and monolithic black stone, however their dating hasn't been established.

I-7b: Tiles with engravings of Gods and Goddesses in the open.

What caused the downfall

There is no recorded history about the downfall or any damage, but that doesn't mean that the place has been left out by the intruders of faith-haters. The state of the temple complex is proof of that. Ignorance and negligence have been the largest contributors.

Current state

The abandoned but revered pieces of faith can be spotted on the ground. The burnt marks can be seen in the corners of the structure. The *yagna*-room is completely out of shape and functionality. The temple complex has been left to oblivion. There are no visitors, no signage, no glimpses into the past of the temple or any historical data displaying any information. The large compound is trespassed on by the public and they do not know the relevance of the complex.

What next

Concrete boundary walls needs to be constructed. A proper fine should be levied for defacing the property. Trespassing and usage of the land for other activities must be fined.

Display boards giving information and historical relevance of the site should be put up. Promoting and listing the complex among the important 'places of visit in Kashmir', should be encouraged.

Kabir felt a strong vibration at the place. One that he hadn't felt so far. He thought that this temple was a living example of the origin and philosophy of the Shiva-Shakti energy, which is so distinct to the Kashmiri way of sprituality The merging of the *panch nags* is akin to how Shiva-Shakti complement each other in creating the universe.

I-8
Loduv Temple
Pulwama

Where in the world would a temple be built in the womb of a sulphur spring? A casual conversation at Nadira's house had prompted Kabir to look for the answer to this question. Intense combing of all online text, essays, and information on temples and monuments built across civilizations, gave him no results. Even telecalls with researchers and professors during those Covid days gave him no leads. Kabir added this to his yellow diary, which was his constant companion throughout his online research—a place where he jotted down all his open issues.

I-8a: The main temple in the middle of a water body.

Loduv temple was revealed to Kabir, when Shakeel casually mentioned how he had frivolously pushed his

10-year-old brother into a sulphur spring, which had a Shiva-linga in the middle. Shakeel was visiting his maternal grandmother, who lived in Pampore and that day both the brothers had marched down 6 km to this temple site to play cricket. Nobody at his grandmother's home knew that they had come so far. This experience from Shakeel set Kabir into motion.

Temple Structure

The 8th century temple is unique in many ways. The first is that it is not on ground level. It is at a lower level. There is a wide fleet of steps, constructed out of limestone, which descend to a water body. In the middle of this water body is the *garbhagriha*.

There are two temples in the complex. The large one stands in the middle of a shallow tank. Water comes to this tank from a spring in the northeast corner of the tank itself. The constant gurgling of the spring water merges seamlessly with the silent and stagnant water of the tank.

Although the temple has a simple structure which is 24 square feet externally, it is different from other temples in Kashmir. It differs both in plan and appearance. There is no decoration on the outside walls. Only the cornice, which consists of three courses of stone adorned with projected fillets, brings some character to the complex. There is a torus course at the base. The corner pilasters are plain and project slightly from the wall. The entrance is headed by a semi-circular, horse-shoe-shaped arch surmounted by a single-storied pediment of a very slight projection. Internally, the temple is circular with a diameter of 17 feet and 6 inches, because of which it resembles the Shankaracharya temple. A plain projecting string course which is at a height of 10 feet from the ground, has a dominical ceiling. Kanjur in lime was used to build the dome and matched it with the ceilings at the Wangath temples (mentioned later in the book).

The roof of the main temple is hollow. The clear blue sky is visible from the circular womb. Inside the circular temple structure, there are many idols and titles with sculptured figures of Gods and Goddesses seen resting on the wall. Likewise, on the outer side of the rectangular temple structure, many broken titles, stone pieces, idols, and sculptured figurines are placed on the base next to the central temple structure. Inside the structure, there is a Shiva-linga.

In the inner wall of the temple, there are holes and mortices, which archaeologists think were meant for scaffoldings while the temple was under construction. But within these circular walls, the base is waterlogged with the tank or spring water. There are again many chiselled divine figures which lay submerged in this water.

The water tank is only a few inches deep but a few green fish of remarkable light and transparency are always seen swimming gracefully in it.

This temple was perhaps the oldest example of Kashmiri medieval architecture. Some researchers also state that the simple structure of Loduv was a prototype of the elaborate style which culminated at Martand and Avantipura.

At the backside of a nearby mosque and a few yards behind this big temple high up on a hill is another temple. This one is smaller in appearance. Externally they look alike, the only difference being that in one of the temples the projecting predicament which encloses the round-headed doorway is developed into a well-defined portico with a trefoil niche. From this arrangement, there is but a single step to the full trefoil-headed recess or entrance enclosed in a steep pediment which is a universal feature of the medieval religious edifices of Kashmir. The portico of this temple has a trefoil arch of which the lower courses are still extant.

There is a base for the sculpture to be placed on. Internally, the temple area is only 6 square feet but the ceiling consists of three courses of overlapping stones. The corner pilaster projects are surmounted by rectangular capitals which seem to have originally borne in relief the figures of probably a lion standing back to back. These corner pilaster projects are not more than 2 inches and the capitals of the pilasters of the portico are carved with floral scrolls.

I-8b: Broken image of a divine figure lying outside.

Material used

Limestone and kankar are the common construction materials used for building both the big and the small temples.

What caused the downfall

There hasn't been enough data to support the causes of the downfall. Even the ruler or the king who commissioned the construction of this temple is not known to historians.

Current state

The temple is now in a muck of water. Dirt and mud sludge have accumulated at the bottom of the tank. There is trash floating on the water's surface. There is filth at numerous places in the complex. The idols and decorated tiles are under layers of moss and dirt.

Muslims still visit the premises to pay their obeisance to the spring which is holy to their faith too. This synergy between the two faiths is beautiful to witness.

A vista of tall chinar trees around the temple complex has maintained the remaining beauty of the place. There is a beautiful mosque next to the temple complex. And a little far ahead is the cave of Nund Rishi, a disciple of the mystic Shaiv poetess of Kashmir, Lalleshwari. The natives believed that Nund Rishi had meditated inside this cave for many years.

What next

Although the temple site is under ASI and they have put up the quintessential signboard giving all the historical and architectural information, yet there is a lot to be done. The complex wears a completely deserted look. The inner and the outer walls are crying for attention.

The idols, the beautifully crafted wall and roofs need serious restoration. The complex has to be made prominent and accessible to people who are inclined to know about the history of Kashmir.

Amongst all the temples that Kabir had visited, this particular temple wretched his heart the most. His diary had no notes that day. No scribbles. No short notes. No reference points. He had all of it secured in his heart. The experience was etched in his heart forever and wasn't going to get erased soon.

I-9
Mamaleshwar Temple
Anantnag

Kabir was on a break from touring around. He needed some time to sort out the information he had collected so far. His diaries looked like an Iranian carpet, full of details and intricacies. He had lost a count of the number of sticky notes pasted on the many notebooks he owned. Each sticky note was colour coded, where each colour represented a certain categorization.

This young researcher usually liked to whip things in shape, but in most situations his mood swings drove the cause. There were days when currency notes in his wallet were arranged to the last denomination and then again there were days when dollars and rupees would get mixed up in the various pockets and pouches, one could think of.

This weekend Kabir was expecting his department senior. As per the last conversation, his University senior David had planned to stay a few days in Srinagar, visit a few tourist spots, and then head back. Kabir spent his entire Friday clearing up the room but upon arrival, David had different plans; he was keen on visiting Pahalgam, the 'valley of the shepherds' and the ancient temple of Mamaleshwar. While Pahalgam was a leisure trip, Mamaleshwar temple, located amidst the dense blue pines and Himalayan spruce, was purely an academic trip.

"Kabir, do you know how the temple got its name?" asked David.

Kabir replied with confidence.

"Well! That's because it's located in a village called Mam Mal. It is next to a stream named Kohaloi, located uphill," replied Kabir.

"Very well, you are close to it, Kabir," said David.

The temple is located on a slope of a ridge and from that point an enchanting panoramic view of Pahalgam is captivating.

Temple Structure

I-9: Temple with two fluted columns.

The temple structure is small and is located on the right side of the roaring Lidder river. Mamaleshwar is not a large-scale temple but it has a place of reverence amongst the devotees.

King Jayasimha (1128–1155) is credited with this temple. *Rajatarangini* mentions this temple as Mammeshvara. It is popular by the names of Mammal and Mamalak as well.

King Jayasimha had adorned the temple with a golden finial. Over time, the structure shows sign of decay. There is an absence of projection in the corner pilaster. A thick coat of lime plaster must have been the cover on the outer surface of the temple. It contains an old staircase that leads to the Shiva-linga inside. This Shiva-linga also finds a mention in the *Rajatarangini*. Right in front of the temple is a spring that oozes from under the temple. This basin which is 12 square feet in measurement, occupies the fore areas of the temple. Water in this tank stays hot in winter and cold in summer. Towards the north of the temple, there is a foundation of a boundary wall. Although there is nothing left of the large boundary wall, yet the remains are visible.

The temple area is 8 square feet internally. It has a porch in the front which supports two fluted columns, one of which is missing. The superstructures have fallen and no remnants of the ceiling are visible. The absence of a ceiling puts Mamaleshwar in the same architectural design as Narasthan.

The shrine finds a mention in Amreshvarakalpa, which proves its remote antiquity.

Material used

Like most other temples of Kashmir, this one is also built out of stones. These blue-shaded stones are locally called *devir kaane*. They are enormous in size with motifs and designs on them.

What caused the downfall

Sikandar Butshikan, 'the Iconoclast', had gone up to Lidder Valley (the valley where the temple is built), intending to break the ice linga at Amarnath and, later proceed towards Mammal, with the intent of breaking the stone Shiva-linga. On reaching Ganeshbal, which is a site for a Ganesh temple and is located at Lambodari or Lidder river, Sikandar broke the stone image of Ganesh. It is said that when the knee of the image was struck with a hammer, a flood of blood flowed down. Sikandar was terrified to see this frightful sight and hence desisted from further destruction of Hindu temples and images. It is believed that after this incident, he abandoned the idea of going ahead to Amarnath cave and Mammal.

Hence, Mamaleshwara temple escaped any sort of destruction but still remained in oblivion. It was not a popular site and only those who were visiting Pahalgam for recreational purposes may have visited the temple, only if they discovered the structure.

Some research papers claim that Shamsudin Araqi, a court member in the kingdom of Herat, had a chance to travel to Kashmir. Upon observing that the Hindus were deeply rooted in 'idolatry', he changed his purpose of staying in Kashmir and began the destruction of all temples and idols.

Current state

The gold *amalaka* (the crowing portion of the spire) has of course disappeared. The outer surface is dull and worn out with time. Certain places and corners are broken and chipped. However, the temple inside is without any damage. The place is still and calm, as it must have been ages ago. Most visitors coming to Pahalgam would not come to this temple as the mule owners have their fixed tourist spots. Therefore, this temple spot usually gets missed by visitors.

What next

It can still be a beautiful venue for many cultural activities. A light and sound show, showcasing the history and ethical richness of Kashmir can attract many visitors to this ancient place. The beauty of the lofty Pahalgam valley will add more charm to the event.

Due to the paucity of time, Kabir hadn't called his family in a long time. Ironically that night, he read a message from his father saying: 'If you find time, do visit the Mamaleshwara temple. It is 3 km from Pahalgam and dates back to 400 AD. When Goddess Parvati created Ganesha out of turmeric and other herbs, she posted him at the gate to guard anyone against going inside, while she takes a bath in the present-day spring. Ganesha, who was her doorkeeper, did not even allow Shiva to enter in and kept saying, "Don't go". He did not allow anyone to enter without Mother Parvati's permission. In our Kashmiri language, this is translated as "Mam Mal", and thus it is known as Mammal temple.' Kabir was excited to share his experience with his father and wondered how the Universe aligns and plans things so seamlessly.

I-10
Manasbal Temple
Ganderbal

Visit to Manasbal temple was not originally on the research list. It became a research point by pure destiny. Kabir and Shakeel were like chalk and cheese. If Shakeel liked the buzz of city life, Kabir wished to stay away from the humdrum of urban chaos. If Shakeel loved to drench himself in the Mumbai showers, Kabir would laze for days on end in the still and creepy silence of the forest. Their friendship had an interesting and Kashmiri start at one of the cafés of Bangalore. And it was this Kashmiri connection which they code-named '*Kandurvaan*'.

It was on one particular weekend that Shakeel chose to be the lotus eater along with Kabir and they took off to Manasbal Lake. Strangely so, because before this Shakeel had never accompanied Kabir to any of his wanderings.

A small wicker basket jostling with hot kehwa, the quintessential *kandurvaan* baked bread, a few jam bottles, and Amul chip-let butter packets, was enough to sustain the long hours in the wilderness of nature.

"Did you know that there is a canal running from the Sindh river? It was built by Zain-ul-Abidin. Are you aware of it?" quizzed Kabir.

Shakeel was still like a stone. His gaze was fixed on the blue sky and the wonders of the universe.

"Yes. It is called the Shahkul canal," quipped Shakeel.

Kabir looked out in the direction of the canal. It was built only a few yards away, on a hilltop. Although it was of no particular interest but due to the beauty of the lake, people of all walks would often crowd this place.

Temple Structure

At the southeast corner of the lake of Manasbal is a miniature temple built of stones. It stands in the middle of the water. Researchers assume that the temple is built in a square of six feet and has only one doorway to the west which is covered by a pediment. This pediment is divided into two portions by a horizontal return of the said moulding, as can be seen in the Martand (mentioned later in the book) colonnade. Only two pyramidal portions are visible in the driest season. The cornice of the lower roof and the horizontal band which divides it from the upper story are decorated with a series of dentils and metopes. The upper part of the pediment which is invisible, faces the west. Only the top of the partially submerged structure is visible.

I-10a: Top of the partially submerged temple.

I-10b: Old picture of the temple surrounded by marshy land.

The top of the temple has a human figure on it, which is holding a staff in the left hand. The angles of the lower portion of the doorway pediment are occupied each with a naked figure leaning against the head of the trefoil. This is placed below the horizontal mounding and above the trefoil. A sort of waving scarf can be seen passing through it.

This temple was built in the 8th or 9th century under the reign of King Avantivarman or King Sankaravarman. But according to noted archaeologist Dr R.C. Agarwal, the Manasbal temple was built by King Jayasimha, who had reigned between 1128 and 1155 in Kashmir.

Material used

The entire temple is made of local grey stone, like the one used at Avantipura temples. Built out of mammoth boulders, the joints of the stones were put together by limewater. The same technique has also been used at the Wangat temple structure. At certain places, the use of steel dowels can be seen, as was used at the Martand temples too. The temple is a fine display of ashlar masonry.

What caused the downfall

There has been no recorded history or hearsay about any sort of invaders or any natural calamity, causing any damage to the temple site. The largest contributor to its current state has been ignorance on part of the concerned authorities, the cold-shoulder from state and central agencies, vagaries of nature, the ignorance of the natives and the continued neglect since so many centuries This temple has never been talked about in public forums.

Current state

Other than the lake area, there aren't many visitors to the temple as such. Due to a lack of maintenance, the temple complex is in a pitiable state. A wrought iron boundary wall protects the spring and the sanctum inside. A few signboards pitched by the authorities are all that can be seen near the main sanctum.

What next

Restoration, repairing, and reclaiming are a few things that the ASI needs to undertake. The history and past of these temple sites have a huge impact on the cultural history of Kashmir and the cultural agencies should encourage people and researchers to explore and bring out their detailed work on it.

Targeted research on the ancient facts and history of the temple can be funded and encouraged. These works have a huge influence on how the future gets shaped.

Shakeel shared a folklore with Kabir, "Do you know that long ago, a saint tied one end of his matted hair with a rope made out of hay and anchored that rope to a nearby tree and jumped into the deep Manasbal Lake? He desired to see the other end of the water, but unfortunately, he never returned to the land."

Kabir was baffled at the amount of courage that the saint must have exhibited to perhaps see the Shiva-linga underwater.

I-11
Martand Temple
Anantnag

It was during the Covid times, that Kabir had for the first time seen the Martand temple in the movie *Haider*. The protagonist was full of anger and spitting venom in a dance form that was shot in the temple compound. The dance troupe appeared minuscule in the presence of the massive temple structure in the backdrop. Kabir was impressed but he thought that the director could have utilized the Sun temple backdrop for a more progressive and positive movie plot.

I-11a: The grand colonnade entrance of the temple.

Later when Kabir was on the premise, he felt the grandness of the temple. Everything else looked so worthless and meaningless in front of the magnificent temple structure. He was confounded by the marvel in limestone and thought to himself: "I will have to plan enough days for a detailed tour of this temple."

In ancient books, this temple is popular by the name of Martandeshwar. The temple commands a magnificent view. It is constructed on a lofty plateau, which once was witness to a beautiful intersection of rivers, lakes, canals, and a cluster of villages. The presence of mighty snow-clad mountains in the backdrop adds to the beauty. There is much speculation regarding the date of construction of this temple and the worship to which it was appropriate. The period of its erection has been between 370 and 500 AD. It is recorded in the *Rajatarangini* as the famous work of King Lalitaditya Muktapida, who had reigned during the 8th century. But in the same book again there are references to the temple being built by King Ranaditya who reigned in the 3/4th century. The book goes on to say that Queen Amrita Prabha, wife of King Ranaditya built 'Amriteshvara', to the south of the main temple. From all these readings Kabir concluded that the complete complex had three building structures inside:

- The principal temple is dedicated to Martand, the Sun God;
- The small temple to the north named Ranapuraswami is dedicated to Lord Shiva;
- The temple of Amriteshvara, is in the south.

Temple Structure

Besides being a *tirtha* of unparalleled relevance during ancient times, this temple is an engineering marvel. Like most other temples of Kashmir built around medieval times, Martand temple has a courtyard with the principal shrine in the middle and a colonnaded peristyle. The courtyard that surrounds the temple is remarkable. It is thought that the interior of the quadrangle was filled with water to a level of one foot of the base of the column. Access to the temple was gained by a raised pathway of slabs supported on solid blocks at short intervals, which connected the gateway flight of steps with those leading to the temple. The same kind of pathway stretched right across the quadrangle from one side doorway to the other. A constant supply of water from river Lidder was enabled through a canal. The temple is not more than 40 feet high but the solid walls and bold outlines, towering over the 84 fluted pillars give an imposing appearance. The latter is 220 feet long and 142 feet broad and faces the courtyard. The peristyle is plain except on the west side which originally had a row of columns similar to the Avantipura temples. The number 84 is accounted sacred by the Hindus in a sequence of it being a product of days in a week and the number of signs in the zodiac.

The temple is divided into three distinct chambers—the outermost is called *ardhamandapa,* meaning *half-temple* measuring 361 square feet, the middle one is called *antarala,* or mid-temple measuring approximately 72 square feet and the innermost is called *garbhagriha* and measures 252 square feet. *Ardhamandapa,* as the name suggests, is highly decorated, the middle chamber is also decently decorated but the last chamber is plain. On the walls of the *antarala,* River-Goddess Ganga is seen standing on her vehicle, the crocodile that is looking up at her. She is bedecked with a double conical tiara and is seen flaunting her regular emblems like the water pot and the stalk of a lotus flower. On her right is a lady holding an umbrella for her and on her left is a *chauri*-bearer. On her opposite is the River-Goddess Yamuna, seated on her vehicle tortoise. Atop the north wall, above the niche is a pair of Gandharvas in flight with an umbrella over them. Vishnu bedecked with coronets is represented on the western wall of the antechamber. Garlanded, Varaha (boar avatar), and Narasimha (man-lion) are shown representing eight arms, and both their hands are placed on the heads of the *chauri*-bearers. On the northern wall again, the bust of Goddess-Earth Prithvi can be seen. A total of 37 images of Gods and Goddesses appear to be on the walls of the temple. Interestingly, on the north-eastern corner shrine is an inscription in Sharada script, the translation to which is not very clear as it is damaged. This dates to be from the 9th century.

This monumental building is dedicated to the worship of the Sun lord and is 75 feet in height, 33 feet in length, and the same in width including the wings. The temple is 63 feet in length and 37 feet in width on the eastern side, and on the western side, it

I-11b: Old picture of people attending a festival in the temple complex.

is 27 feet in width. The walls of the temple are 9 feet thick and the entrance chamber is 4 feet thick. The entrance was through a wide flight of steps. On each of the other sides was a closed doorway surmounted by a trefoiled arch, and covered by a pediment that rose to a height of 60 feet. On each side of the doorway angles, stout pilasters were divided into panels, each decorated with a miniature Aryan-style temple. These pilasters supported the entablatures, and hence gave full strength to the vast and massive roof. This lofty pyramid of stone was broken into two portions separated by an ornamental band and is decorated with small niches with pointed roofs and trefoiled recesses.

The peristyle is the largest of its kind in the entire Kashmir valley. The quadrangle contained 70 round fluted pillars, 10 square parallel pillars, and 4 pillars in the central porch. In the middle of the larger side, there is a pair of fluted pillars that are 13 feet in height and 9 feet in width apart.

Each of the pillars is 9 feet in height, and 21 feet in diameter and has an intercolumniation of 6 feet 9 inches. The imposts were surmounted by human-headed birds facing each other and a single bird looking ahead.

The entrance stands in the middle of the western side of the quadrangle and is of the same width as the temple itself. This proportion is in accordance with the grandeur of the Hindu architecture—which emphasizes on giving different proportions of the width of the temple for each different style of gateway from the most simple to the most magnificient. The complex is open in the west and east directions. The inner and outer porticos are divided by a cross wall, which may have had a wooden door.

Each flank of the pediment of the gateway is supported by an 8 feet high massive fluted pillar. One of these still stands to the south of the entrance. The style of the architrave and the entablature which connected the pillars with the gateway is similar to the Avantiswami temple. Researchers believe that the front and back pediments of the gateway were supported on similar large pillars. Further adding to their conclusions—the square foundation in the front may be the remains of the wing walls of the flight of steps, and the roof may be pyramidal. The walls of the gateway, both internal and external, are heavily decorated with rows of double-pedimented niches and altered with the rectangular panel. The pedimented niches contain single-standing figures of Gods or an amorous group, similar to those at Avantipura. Two large niches on the side walls of the inner chamber contain tall figures of three-headed Vishnu standing between two attendants, whereas the rectangular panel contains the sitting groups, floral scrolls, pairs of geese, etc. Below the Vishnu panel is a large panel decorated with a row of dancing urchins displaying different expressions.

The other sides of the quadrangle are ornamented by a succession of trefoil-headed panels similar in shape and size to the recessed opening of the interior. Archaeologists infer from the remains that the western façade was adorned by a series of columns, similar to that of the two temples in Avantipura.

Some of the historical books showed that the Sun temple was probably of an earlier date. It is possible that King Arya Raja (360–383 AD), along with Buddhist Prince Meghavahan (383–400 AD), may have possibly built this temple before anyone else. Both these kings were rich predecessors of King Ranaditya and worshippers of Shiva.

Another revelation, which had been stated by earlier historians also came to the fore. Prior to the construction of the present temple, there existed another temple but of a smaller dimension at the same site. During the construction of the new temple, the previous old temple base was maintained as it is and a new temple structure that enveloped the old base was built on. This can be confirmed by the existence of both bases, side by side, one within the other on the east side of the temple. The old base must be the one built by King Ranaditya.

Material used

The entire temple is made of grey limestone and gigantic boulders. The logistics of ferrying, lifting, and placing these enormous stones is beyond human comprehension.

What caused the downfall

According to historian Jonaraja, the temple complex was dismantled by Sikandar Butshikan. This was part of his plan to convert all Hindus and bring down all the Hindu temples. The idols inside the temple were vandalized and even the remains are not visible now. Some historians believe that the present condition of the temple is caused by an earthquake that hit the valley in the 14th century.

This claim is contradicted by Suka, another historian who in his book *Chaturtha Rajatarangini*, mentions that the *tirthas* of Vijeshwara, Martand, and Varahshetra were not impacted by the 14th century earthquake.

Current state

Unfortunately, the hands of most of the images have broken. The emblems in their hands are beyond recognition. Much of the carvings on the walls have been vandalized and at some places, the structure is weathered out.

Disregard and negligence for many centuries by all the ruling governances has seized the dues to the monument. It is a mass of lifeless stones.

During excavation, a vast quantity of debris and stones were removed. Many earthen pots and jars were discovered embedded in the floor of the courtyard. Many other valuable artifacts were discovered from beneath the rubble, some of which are now well-preserved in the museum, and some had been stolen.

What next

Martand should be listed among the must-visit sun temples of India. It should be listed along with Konark, Modhera, and other such important temples. Restoration and preservation of the structure is the responsibility of the State and the Central ruling agencies, of the existing civil society that lives there and the guardians of the culture of Kashmir.

In recent times a movie was shot on the premises and a religious event was also organized. This should be encouraged more often, without causing any damage to the site.

A few other suggestions could be:

- Hosting movie shows;
- Hosting book and literary events;
- Hosting cultural events;
- Hosting a theatrical, showcasing the history of Kashmir;
- Kiosk providing small write-ups about the temple through a brochure, etc.

During his exhaustive research, Kabir understood that each *tirtha* or temple in Kashmir had a Mahatmya attached to it, which is a venerated narration in praise and glory of the *tirtha*. Similarly, there was a Martand Mahatmya too. While he was reading through the translation of the script, he recalled the *puranic* story of the origin and name of Martand, that his grandmother had narrated to him. According to the story, Aditi the wife of Rishi Kashyap, had given birth to 13 children. The earlier 12 are Aditya, Ravi, Ghabasti, Bhanu, Divakara, Savita, Garma, Tapan, Bhaskar, Surya, Tvasta, and Surapati. The thirteenth child was thrown in Satisar Lake by Aditi. Rishi Kashyap with the blessing of the Trident broke the mountain, and a gush of river Vitasta flowed. In the water body, Rishi Kashyap found the egg and held it in his hands. The luminous egg illuminated the surroundings with its vibrant aura. Thus emerging from this lifeless egg (*mṛtta aṇḍa*), emerged the mighty Sun and the grandiose temple of Martand.

The surya mandala, which Kabir's grandmother would make at the entrance of their house in the month of

June (the seventh day of Asadh as per the lunar calendar) became fresh like yesterday in his memory.

Even the Mughal emperor Akbar was spellbound by the imposing Martand temple and had gifted cows adorned with gold and pearls to the Brahmins of Martand.

I-12

Naaranag Temple

Ganderbal

Naaranag was not even on Kabir's list of temples to research. He had entered the last phase of his exploration and was mapping his beta readings against the *Rajataringini*. It was the lines in canto 107 and 347 of *Tarang I*; canto 123 and 139 of *Tarang II* and canto 189 in *Tarang IV* that caught his attention. They were talking about a certain *nag*, also called Sodarnag or Narannag. There is a repeat mention of Bhuteshwara or Bhutesha (all forms of Lord Shiva) by Kalhana in *Rajatarangini*. Kalhana further goes on to say that this huge temple complex was patronized by various Hindu rulers of Kashmir.

I-12a: Dismantled structure of the main temple.

To the true nature of a scholar, Kabir dug further into the *Nilamata Purana,* to verify if these findings found a mention in other books of those times. The *Nilamata Purana* has repeatedly mentioned Bhuteshwar Teertha or Soodarnag or Soodarteertha in its text. This meant that there was another unexplored temple waiting to be revealed to the world.

He put a pause to all his compilations and set out to Naaranag, which is also mentioned as Wangath in ancient books. Naaranag branches off from the Sonamarg highway. The road towards Naaranag goes through Kangan, a town in the district of Ganderbal.

Across the river, the mountain slope is infested with dense pine trees which give a clustered view of the evergreen surface of tree tops. The stone fall silence echoes in and around the expanse and works as a kind of sedative for divine practices.

The murmuring cool breeze through cones of evergreen trees spread a canopy of coolness in the atmosphere. And the fuzzy slope over which the structure was raised too has a long string of lush green forest along the descent of the mountain in the back. The temple site was nestled in the womb of this fabulous bloom.

Temple Structure

The complete complex is massive. From a bird's eye view, it appears like a mess of boulders and stone slabs. There is a big temple structure in the centre and then there are small temple structures in the compound. Three main groups of temple structures were built for three forms of Lord Shiva, namely Bhuteshwara, Jyeshtharudra, and

Muthas. These were constructed around 220 BC by King Jaluka.

There are two huge temple structures here. Both are at a distance of approximately 200 metres and are surrounded by the thick foliage of fir and willow trees.

The temple complex has an idyllic location; it is placed in the dense, dark green forest of fir and pine trees in the lap of the Harmukh Mountains. The mountain slopes are steep and notorious for safe human ascend. It is haunted by jungle bears who ravage the place for ripe maize in the early autumn season. The foamy and torrential Sindh river flowing next to the temple complex is in clear contrast to the quiet forest around. The stretch behind has the trail to the arduous and steep Gangabal pilgrimage.

For anyone to reach this cluster of temples, Kangan is the destination they should put on the map. According to ancient Puranas, Wangat or Vangat was known as Vashishth Ashram after Sage Vashishth. Many Hindus believe that he had stayed here and consecrated the shrine of Jyeshtharudra.

Naaranag owes its name to the numerous springs situated in and around the temple complex. Built during the medieval period there is no symmetry in the way and the distances at which these clusters have been built. Judging by the position, the six temples are within an enclosed boundary wall. There is a remarkable difference in the archaeological design of these temples, they indicate that they had been built during different periods. Researchers believe that the existence of many springs must have attracted sanctity to this place.

The main temple area is 25 square feet. This is similar in many ways to the other temples of Kashmir. Except for a few features; it is not structured in a vimana style, which has all four sides open. But this one has two entrances, opposite to each other on the northeast and southwest sides. The second difference is the doomed ceiling, although from the outside the roof is pyramidal. The ceiling is built out of circular courses of kanjur stone. It is crowned at the apex of a full-blown lotus. The dome which cuts off the angles formed by the walls, springs from four large cornerstones. In the centre of the floor is an unpaved square shape. It marks the site of the pedestal of the picture. The mortices of the tenons of the doors can still be seen in both entrances. On two sides of the string course upon which the dome is placed, eight rectangular slots hold the rafter of the canopy over the image.

The closed sides of the temple are externally decorated with square-topped recesses. Each of these display pedestal of an image which is probably a replica of the one in the sanctum. The core of the roof consists of rubble stone masonry in lime. Aurel Stein has identified this temple with the Shiva-Jyeshtharudra temple of Lalitaditya.

Another temple located close to the above temple possesses gaps on three sides intended for an image. Their pedestal with tenons is *in situ*. Part of the top of the kanjur wall is intact. The temple immediately touching the porch of the preceding shrine is a single square structure, plain both internally and externally. The ceiling is not dominical and has been built with overlapping stones. This is validated by the only stone *in situ*.

Behind this is the basement of another small temple, but the superstructure of this has fallen. Its ceiling is overlapping.

Next to this one, there are two other temples. Opening to one is in the north-east and other is south-east direction respectively. The ceiling for this temple was dominical.

The gateway of the chamber is located in the northwest corner and not in the middle of the wall. It is a two-chambered structure. In each chamber are the bases of two columns that support the porch's roof. Fragments of the column are now strewn around the area. The retaining wall of the plinth is built of closely packed pieces of slate. They look beautiful and compact.

A broad causeway leading to the second set of temples which is situated at about two hundred metres is constructed out of granite.

I-12b: The entire temple complex with many small structures.

And in between all these half-fallen and half-standing temples, there is a huge pile of rocks, boulders, and blocks that lay astray on the ground, to which only the plinth is standing. They can be categorized into another set of temples. The residual hint at an erstwhile *baradari* or a pillared hall which may have been about 100 feet long and 67 feet broad. The bases of the column are *in situ*. They are eight on the longer side and four on the shorter side. Between the central pair of columns, a staircase is built, which is facing the first set of temples. A slot in the landing area of the top of the stairs looks to have been intended for holding the post of screens. Sumahanas Rilhana's brother, the minister in King Jayasimha's court had built a congregation hall or a *matha*. It is assumed that the *baradari* is the same *matha*.

The lower group of temples is enclosed in a massive rectangular stonewall pierced by two-chambered gateways. It is sad to see the half-buried and half-strewed structures inside the enclosed wall. The largest is the temple of Siva-Bhuteshvara. In size, it is similar to the first set of temples. Internally, it is 17 square feet in area. In the south, there are two small shrines. The first one is built in small pieces of slate in lime mortar, placed on a granite base. The second has an immense rectangular stone trough carved out of a single massive granite stone. Inside the wall, there is a small temple that has a round entrance.

Many pieces of craftsmanship lay around the entire complex. A Shiva-linga on an octagonal pedestal in the southeast of the quadrangle and two beautiful geese decorated in the corner of the same quadrangle have a stunning appearance.

In the northwest corner of the peristyle is a huge spring. The water, some say comes from the Gangabal point and flows into the tank through the masonry wall. The water is cool and sweet, and houses a lot of fish. Slightly higher up, is a temple of which, only the pyramid is visible since the rest of it has been buried underneath.

A long line of brick masonry on the enclosure wall is debris of the cellular quadrangle, usually common in Kashmiri temples. These massive granite stones are of extraordinary size. And each stone is finely carved and juxtaposed. Each block of boulder must have been shaped with much painstaking effort and immense patience and care. The boundary wall had to be of strength since they were the first-level guards towards the mighty mountains at the back.

A visit to these temples for devotees was sacrosanct after the holy pilgrimage to Gangabal. Hindus visited Gangabal to immerse the ashes of the deceased. The priest in charge of Naaranag was usually in a supreme commanding position. This was so largely because the temple had a huge estate.

During his reign, when King Lalitaditya went on world conquest, he took some reserve from the Bhuteshwar temple and after returning victorious, he paid back eleven times what he had borrowed from the temple treasury.

Around the water body, there are many Shiva-lingas, and each is installed by different ministers and citizens of honour. King Lalitaditya's friend Mitrasharman, installed Mitreshwar-Linga, similarly, a teacher named Bhapata installed the Bhapateshwar-Linga in the Naaranag complex.

The locality of temples nearer to Naaranag is known as Rajdainbal. It is enclosed by a wall measuring 176 feet long and 130 feet wide. This group consists of six buildings, most of which are ruined and devastated now. The main block is surmounted by a rubble pyramidal roof, and the gables which terminated the porch-like projections on all four sides can still be traced. This is in a better position and can be entered from the eastern and the western sides.

The dome and roof are of masonry and both maintain their original and pyramidal form. Among the large dump of stones, is a stone column of huge dimension, and is so weather-worn that with great difficulty it is established that they are fluted for simple rounded columns. The doorways and side recesses show detailed carving but the signs of a violent conquest are so vivid that no definite form can be traced.

Material used

A large quantity of lime has been used in the masonry of the temple. Kanjur stone, rubble stone, granite stone, grey granite stone, and large rock pieces have been used in the construction of the temple. Each stone of mammoth size has been shaped with vigilant care and utmost patience.

What caused the downfall

After the death of Avantivarman, which was during the later medieval period, these temples faced misfortune. The temple treasury was plundered by Bhadravesvara, a minister of Samagramraja (1003–1028 AD). Again, a conflagration under the reign of Uchchala (1101–1111 AD), caused a lot of damage to the building. A group of 'hill men' were ordered by a rebel baron Hayavadana to marauder the temples.

Moss, in growth vegetation, stone reactions, ruthlessness of time, etc. have created havoc on the ancient monument.

Current state

It is all in ruins now. The site is one big place of rubble and dismantled stone structures. The causes of the destruction are both man-made and nature-made. Inroads of vegetation can be seen across the half-standing temples. And there is graffiti on certain inner walls of a few of the temples. Layers of green moss are visible along the edges of the building. Weathering and denudation due to climatic changes have weakened the comprehensive strength of the stone.

These buildings are pieces of art and history but unfortunately are under no preservation or maintenance.

Locals visit this place as a picnic spot. This brings a good footfall to the site, but it needs to be managed better. The visiting people should be trained to be conscious about preserving and not littering the place. The green patches around are a beautiful spot to pause and admire the mountain range around, but more importantly, the site has to be maintained as a historical monument and not as an amusement park.

What next

A boundary wall and an information board is the least ASI can come up with. There is tremendous work needed at the site:

- Since the temple has been constructed by different rulers over different periods, the name tag of the builder should be put against each temple rubble.
- As is the case for all ancient temples of Kashmir, the local guides need to be trained with the correct history. Any misinformation can do more harm than any good.
- Trash bins are essential. The site is littered at many places with garbage.
- Promotion of the place through events, which would attract scholars and researchers.

Kabir's closing notes in the diary were heart-wrenching.

> *My heart bleeds to see how time and humans together have made a mockery of the great craftsmanship that human beings had created centuries ago. King Jayendra (61 BC) would come here to worship Bhuteshvara. King Lalitaditya had built a stone pedestal with silver conduit at this shrine for the bathing of the sacred images. The great historian Kalhana and his father Canpaka were frequent visitors to this sacred tirtha. But, then what happened to this holy place of immense positive energies that everyone turned a blind eye and left it to be just another touristy place in Kashmir, where people dump and litter the wrappers of FMCGs on a historic site which is older than the forefathers of the generation living there today?*

I-13

Narasthan Temple

Pulwama

Kabir disembarked from his caravan and rested his glance at the splendid temple standing in front of him. Narasthan temple, located 20 miles northeast of Avantipura, was a 'must-visit' on his list. After a rough but pleasant journey from Ganderbal, Kabir was all set to explore the temple complex.

With the first step in the premise, a current passed through his spine. A magnificent erstwhile structure which was built approximately 1,400 years ago, was left in shambles now. He stooped further to pass through the small entry gate of the temple, which was now only a frame made of four courses of stone. The original boundary wall must have been five feet wide and five feet tall. Interestingly, the absence of this boundary wall has made the gate look big.

Kabir was aware that the temple was commissioned in the 6th or the 7th century by the valiant ruler King Lalitaditya Muktapidya. King Lalitaditya is remembered as the world conqueror, and his reign ranged from present-day Afghanistan to parts of present-day South India. Besides many military conquests, the great king has many temples and sanctuaries to his credit. Kabir remembered his grandmother narrating the gallant stories of the great King Lalitaditya. Narasthan is this valiant king's gift to society.

Kabir strolled around the cella and remembered that during a video call with his local friend, he had observed that the temple did not have a ceiling. As a student of history and ancient monuments, this was a first-of-a-kind temple he had witnessed.

In the picturesque womb of the lofty Brariangan range, stands Narasthan (place of Narayan). This temple was a place of worship for Lord Vishnu, but, during an excavation work undertaken by English writer W.R. Lawrence, there were specimens of other sculptures too.

Temple structure

I-13a: View from the entrance of the temple compound.

The entire temple courtyard measures about 70 square feet. The entrance to the temple is from the west side of the complex through an imposing portico. The outer portal is arched and one can see designs of Aryan architecture on the pediment. It is supported by two columns about eight feet high and the width between the columns is about four and a half feet. At the top of the pediment, there is a figure carved, which resembles a Garuda—half man and half eagle. Garuda is considered to be the king of birds and has the power to acquire any shape. The outer vestibule measures about 8 feet by 4 feet; in the middle is a square gateway opening into the second vestibule of rather larger dimensions.

In the centre of the complex is the main temple. The base of the main temple rests on four courses of stone. The cornice is a plain, straight-lined, filleted course, of which only the top fillet is rounded off into a cyma recta moulding. The corner pilasters project slightly from the temple walls and the base rests on a square structure. Amongst the other distinctions of the temple, the absence of a very common circumambulatory path on top of the base and the trefoil arches on the peripheral shrine walls, makes Narasthan stand out from other temples. The circumambulatory path which is a common feature in the temple bases of most temples in Kashmir is missing here. For the trefoil arches, the process has been reversed. Unlike most temples, the lower trefoil encloses a deeply recessed niche whereas the upper arch is shallow and projects only 2 inches from the plain wall surface.

A flight of four steps lead to the shrine of Narasthan. Two swags of beaded garlands are adorned on the pilaster of the side walls of the staircase. In front of the temple stairs, there is a water tank. Water was poured into the tank through an elaborate stone conduit. The spout of the conduit is carved in front with a bloomed lotus through the centre of which the water flows. A grinning crocodile head decorates its sides. On top of the spout is a platform measuring 12 by 6 inches which probably may have served as a bathing area or a cool place for an afternoon siesta. From the tank, a drain takes the water to a chamber from where the water leaves the complex. This chamber approximately 9 by 12 feet, in size probably must have served as a bathroom for female worshippers. Inside, it has a trefoil pediment window measuring one by one foot, sliced on the wall at a height of three feet above the ground.

The portico projects four inches from the temple wall. The inside wall is decorated with a six-armed figure of a Goddess, decorated on each of the two pediment niches. The upper two hands hold a pitcher and a full-blown lotus; the middle seems to be holding the breast, and the lower two hands are hanging downwards but the object they seem to be holding is not visible. Miniature fluted columns are standing on the base and are surmounted by capitals on each side of the niche, which is similar in style to Avantipura. At the bottom, there are three similar niches containing atlantes. Two bird-like figures adorn the capitals of the outer surface.

The main temple cell measures 8 feet by 6 feet in dimension. It faces south and contained a Shiva-linga. The walls are quite plain, except for a string course at a height of seven feet and six inches from the floor, which resembles the cornice of the plinth outside. A small double-pediment niche is placed on the east wall and its upper pediment is decorated with the carved figure of a kneeling human being. The left pilaster of the niche is only half-carved, and this is an evident illustration of the method of work of the ancient sculptors who were accustomed to carving large stone blocks *in situ*. The walls run perpendicular until the level of the eaves is reached, after which they begin to contract. Each course is spanned out narrowly, where finally a finial must have been placed.

In the middle of the three sides of the cell wall, there is an alcove. In the middle of each wall is a trefoil recess surmounted by a high-pitched double pediment. Next to it is a shallow trefoil arch surmounted by a two-storied pediment. On the north and west sides, there is a small square postern. The one in the north measures about three feet by two, whereas the one in the west most likely may have led to a square chamber that occupied the southwest corner of the enclosure. A small arched window throws some light into this chamber. There is another shrine located in the north of this chamber, which has a sloping roof and a ceiling similar to that of the Pandrethan temple (mentioned later in the book).

I-13b: The fragmented boundary walls of the temple.

In the middle of the south wall, there is a gateway. The gateway is opposite to the sanctum and consists of a doorway connecting the two chambers, each measuring seven feet by four feet. This gateway is a double-chambered structure that is open on two sides, for entry and exit. On the outside, the lintel of the doorway is carved with a beautiful design of crenelations and lozenges.

Material used

Originally the temple was built out of greyish limestone and was covered with a thick coat of lime plaster. Over the many centuries the coat has worn off, but traces of the residual can still be spotted in the structure.

What caused the downfall

The monument was devastated by invader Sikander Butshikan, in the 14th century. It stays the way, Sikander Butshikan may have left it many centuries ago. No restoration, repair, order of any sorts has been put at the site by any governing agencies.

Current state

The big boulders, once a part of the temple, now lay astray in the complex. They seem to have stayed that way for centuries now. Creepers and wild grass are visible across the crevices in the temple structure.

One can see the newly constructed residential houses in the backdrop of the temple complex. The new generation of Kashmiris look in awe at the building, but they are yet to value the significance of this monument built by one of the greatest rulers of Kashmir.

The only sigh of relief is that despite the current turmoil in Kashmir, Narasthan temple hasn't been defaced any further. The temple has not been visited for veneration but is frequented by researchers, archaeologists, and researchers for obvious reasons.

What next

Perhaps the State cultural department and other concerned authorities should take up the restoration of the temple. Other than the renewal of the temple, they can put up clear signage, a brief history of the monument, maybe an AI-enabled hypothetical picture of the original structure, and a short introduction of the builder and list the temple to the 'must-visit' destinations in Kashmir. It is an important landmark in the cultural and social history of Kashmir, which should be highlighted.

I-14
Pandrethan Temple
Srinagar

Amongst all the temples of Kashmir, Pandrethan temple has a unique location. It is on the Srinagar-Anantnag highway. It is an ancient shrine constructed out of stone, which stands in the middle of a tank but is surrounded by a grove of willows and Chinar trees.

It is an 8th century temple built by Meruvardhana, who was a minister in the court of King Partha (906–921 AD). He had dedicated himself to the services of Lord Vishnu and thus got the name Vishnu-Meruvardhana. The land on which the temple was constructed was at that time under the occupation of Srinagar city, which was founded by Ashoka, the great king who had ruled over the entire North of India. The modern name Pandrethan is a corruption of the original Sanskrit name titled Puranadhisthana, which means old capital.

But this theory of Vishnu-Meruvardhana is weakened by the presence of a seated figure, which resembles Lakulis'a, a form of Shiva. This Shaivite figure can be found in the trefoil niche above the northern entrance. And even the floor arrangement inside the cella indicates that this must have been a Shiva temple.

Rilhana, a minister under King Jayasimha in 1135 AD had erected a Shiva-Rilhanesvara temple, around the same site.

Temple Structure

I-14a: The leaning temple structure submerged in water.

The temple is 18 feet square with a projecting portico on each side and displays a clear indication of having been built at a later date than other ancient temples in Kashmir. At certain places, there is a repetition of decoration for the sake of exuberance, especially the repetition of pediment within pediment and trefoil within trefoil. The monotony of the roof is relieved by an ornamental band of dentils that divide it horizontally into two parts.

In the upper part of the pyramid are the four trefoil ventilation apertures. The cella is plain except for the ceiling. It consists of nine stones arranged in three overlapping squares, each of which cuts off the angles of the squares below.

The doomed roof is covered with sculptures of classic designs. The pyramidal roof of 12 courses of stone is divided into two portions by an ornamental band. These 12 triangles are thus used for decoration. Each triangle in the lowest square contains a figure of Yaksha, facing each other and holding a garland. The second group of triangles consists of four figures each holding a disc in their right hand and a lotus stalk in their left hand. Flying figures can be seen in the upper group of triangles. A square slab crowns the entire piece, which is decorated with lotus inside a decorated circle. What is noteworthy is how beautifully the human figure has been shown in motion; it looks as though they are swimming, without any appendage of wings. Inside the cella, there is a depression of 7 feet, which probably must have been the place for the deity's image. The floor of the cella is paved with stone flags.

The pilasters at the corner are surmounted by carved capitals. The ceiling is formed by nine blocks of stone: four of which are resting over the angle of the cornice have reduced the opening to a square. The entire ceiling rests on a corbelled course. The corbelled course is inward projecting and is decorated with a row of flowers inside horizontal rows. An upper cornice of four more stones has further reduced the opening, which is covered by a single block and is decorated by a lotus. The temple is built in mandapa style, meaning that it is open on all four sides. There are doorways on each of the four sides, but they open only in the north, east and west directions. Only a window opens in the south direction. The total

I-14b: Old picture with grassy and swampy land around the temple structure.

height from the floor to the ceiling is 15 feet. The load over the ceiling is taken by shallow pyramidal brackets. There is no access to these closed chambers.

The bold projection of the pilaster which supports the pediment of the porches and the retirement of the connecting walls brings a distinct play of light to the temple. The jambs are made of ashlar courses and are faceted, but the sills are plain. It is probably the best example of the true Kashmiri style extant.

Material used

Sandstone blocks have been used to construct the temple. The size is enormous and the filing of the stones is phenomenal.

What caused the downfall

The present city of Srinagar in ancient times was called Pravarapura, probably shortened for Pravarasenapura. Unfortunately, under the rule of Abhimanyu, in about 960 AD, the entire city was engulfed in fire. This blaze was so violent that the entire temple complex was in flames, except for the main sanctum. The water body around the shrine saved it from the fire. Perhaps the whimsical nature of fire and the conqueror who always eyed the rich valley of Kashmir with evil desires caused the extermination of the beautiful temple. Innumerable treasures were discovered during an excavation in the north direction of the temple. During this digging, the foundations of many ancient houses of the old capital of Pravarapura were unearthed. Valuables were discovered, which once again display the rich legacy of Kashmir.

Current state

Due to the after-effect of the earthquake and the cold-heartedness of time, the stone courses of the roof have tilted from their position. Since the dome is declined, it appears as if the edifice is crying over the lost city, of which this is the only last relic. In the neighbourhood, there are fragments consisting of two Shiva-lingas, of which one is six feet tall and the other one is broken into three small pieces. Of the broken pieces, the lower part is polygonal and the upper is round with a conical top. If one was to bring all these pieces together, the total height would have been 16 feet. There is a huge mass of stone near these pieces. They appear to be the feet and legs of an idol and are as high as the knees of a colossal seated figure; most probably it could be a Buddhist image. Charles Baron Hugel, the famous explorer and diplomat, believed that Pandrethan was a Buddhist edifice and mentions that there are well-preserved Buddhist figures inside the temple. But there is a contradicting opinion to this and other scholars claim that Hugel is mistaken, because this is purely a Vishnu temple.

Around the structure, a foundation of a mosque has been built with stones taken from this temple. This mosque is located north of the temple. At present, the temple is maintained and managed by the Army officers of the Badamibagh Cantonment area. The complex is clean and well-maintained but only a few devotees visit the temple now.

What next

Information brochures with the correct historical and cultural information about the venue can be shared with the visiting tourists. Local guides and escorts, who are the cultural ambassadors of Kashmir should be well trained. The temple complex has a huge potential for hosting cultural events, debates, research studies and much more.

More than the Army, it is the responsibility of the State authorities, to ensure that the place is well preserved and maintained.

I-15

Parihasapura Temple

Baramulla

That night Kabir had decided to sleep on the terrace and hence he did not check into any posh hotels in Srinagar. The next morning, the sky was worth a million dollars. He captured the deep azure skies with spots of white clouds in his DSLR.

After a heavy breakfast of kehwa and buttered *bakerkhani,* Kabir hopped into the hired cab and set off towards Baramula road. Shakeel's mother had packed some rice and cooked vegetables in a casserole for Kabir. A humble village named Narbal was located 14 kilometres from Srinagar. Situated here, at an elevation is the erstwhile capital city of Parihasapura, chosen by King Lalitaditya. The plateau of Parihasapura had every advantage over the low and swampy Srinagar. The capital city was changed from Srinagar to Parihasapura and soon it became popular as 'the laughing city'. 'Parihas' in Sanskrit means to laugh and 'Pur' means city.

Kabir walked towards the large expanse of 5 acres of land. As far as his eyes could see, the land was studded with heaps of ruins of the erstwhile capital city. The most prominent amongst them are three Buddhist structures, a stupa and a *chaitya.*

Parihasapura was about 3 kilometres southwest of Shadipur. He remembered his grandmother had visited Shadipur on a pilgrimage, which is at a confluence of the Indus (Sind) and Jhelum (Vitasta) rivers, and is also called Prayag by Kashmiri Pandits. Kabir's friend had suggested that he could take the boat through the idyllic corn fields of Trigam and then ascend a gradual slope to reach Parihasapura, but the visitor refused because he wished to take the road less travelled.

Kabir spotted the oldest *boaen* (Kashmiri name for the Chinar tree), in the middle of the confluence. It was compared by the erstwhile Hindus living in this area with the fig tree of Triveni Sangam, near Allahabad. Even after so many centuries, the locals say that the *boaen* has always been of the same size. It has neither increased nor decreased in size.

Temple structure

I-15a: The giant steps leading to the top of the demolished temple.

This temple has five large buildings:

- the temple of Mukta-Keshava with a golden image of Vishnu;
- the temple of Parihasa-Keshava with an image of Vishnu;
- the temple of Mahavaraha with Vishnu's image clad in golden armour;
- the temple of Gvardhanadhara with a silver image;
- the Rajavihara with a large quadrangle.

The superstructure of the temple is entirely missing. What is left now is only a huge mass of boulder debris, covering the entire top of the plateau. There is a 5-inch-deep circular hole in the middle of a massive boulder, which has been resting in the centre of the plateau for centuries. Probably this stone was a part of the finial of the stupa, and the hole was the mortice in which the staff of the stone umbrella was embedded.

The base of the plateau is 256 square feet in plan, with a flight of steps on each side. Its moulding is a round torus in the middle and there is a filleted torus as the cornice. The pilaster on the railings and the side walls of the steps are decorated with carved figures in standing and sitting atlantes positions. They have the appearance of respectable gentlemen. The top surface of each of the two plinths is amply spaced and broad enough for circumambulation. One can see boulders lying across the southeastern and southwestern corners of the site. A fillet pattern runs through the round torus stones, which probably must have been a part of the string course on the drum of the stupa.

To the south of the stupa is a royal monastery or a *rajavihara*. Through the flight of steps on the eastern side, there is a huge veranda. One can also see fragments of trefoil arches which contain images of Buddha and Bodhisattvas. Researchers claim that these idols were of giant sizes and reached up to the sky.

The complex is a quadrangle structure of 26 cells. These cells which are dilapidated now, run alongside a stone-flag square-shaped courtyard. In front of each cell stood a covered veranda, which was supported by a colonnade. A flight of steps leads to the courtyard. It is assumed that these were the apartments occupied by the abbots of the sanctuary. A stone trough in a nearby corner must have served as a bathing point. A couple of stone drains passing underneath some of the cells may be the conduit to carry off rainwater or excess water from the courtyard. In front of the temple, steps are the base of a column which probably supported the *dhvaja*, bearing the special emblem of the deity enshrined in the sanctuary. The flank walls are decorated with atlantes similar to those of the stupa.

During one of the excavations, it was interesting to find a small earthen jug which contained 45 silver coins in excellent preservation. They belonged to the times of King Vinayaditya, King Vigraha and King Durlabha (rulers during the 7th and the 8th centuries). These finds have been well displayed in the numismatic section of the Srinagar Museum.

The enormous size of the blocks of limestone used in the construction, the smoothness of their dressing, fineness of the joints have been some of the extraordinary features of this complex.

In the south of this building is the *chaitya* which stands on a double base. The entrance to this is through the east side after taking a flight of steps. Fragments of the trefoil arch, which covered the entrance are now lying on the ground. There is the foundation of a small diaper-rubble-style building near the *chaitya*.

The floor of the sanctum is 14 feet by 13 feet by 5 feet. The massive size of the boulders used so long back in Kashmir could only be compared with the building materials used in ancient Egypt. The ceiling of the circumambulatory passage may have been supported by four columns. Now only the bases of the four corners survive, the roof which may have been of the pyramidal type was supported on the massive stone wall of the path. The boundary wall is constructed out of a rubble-stone wall.

Rajatarangini claims that King Lalitaditya constructed a separate stone shrine of Shiva and installed two images of Lord Rama. These images were later unearthed near the village of Suravardhamana.

Material used

The structure is largely built out of limestone. Large and massive stones have been unique to this temple. One can see the different displays of designs in the way the stone walls have been constructed; be it the diaper rubble or the rubble stone or the stone flag. Mobilizing these enormous sizes of blocks of limestone must have been an extraordinary task for the workers back then in the 7th century when technology and machinery were nonexistent. For the first time, gold, copper and silver were used in the construction. Historians claim that 3,600 kg of silver and 62,000 kg of copper were used for the Buddha and Vishnu idols.

I-15b: A defaced human figure on the column.

What caused the downfall

After Lalitaditya's demise, the royal residence fell to the evil plan of his successors. The capital city was moved back to Srinagar. The confluence point of the Vitasta and Sindhu was changed from Parihasapura to the current time Shadipur. This must have seriously impaired the importance of Lalitaditya's favourite city. A century and a half after his death, the exquisite and important material from the shrine was used by the new rulers to build new temples in the town of Pattan. *Rajatarangini* also mentions that during a war, King Harsha was informed that his enemies were hiding in the temple complex of Parihasapura. As a result, he destroyed the entire complex in search of his enemies. Successive invaders seized and melted the massive Buddha idol, and the silver image of Vishnu was subsequently carried away and demolished by evil hands. The final blow to the destruction of the temples of Parihasapura was attributed to Sikander Butshikan (1394–1416 AD), who along with his entire troop invaded the valley.

Current state

One can see a well-defined signage which is placed at a pivot point giving proper direction and location to the visitors. Although the temple does not see any pilgrimage, it has become a popular tourist spot for the locals. One ASI signage reads 'Protect Monument', but a lot of restoration work is required to salvage the lost heritage of the temple complex. As part of restoration work, a few sculptured human and animal figures were constructed, which now have been left halfway. These were constructed in 2010 by the cultural committee.

What next

The temple can be restored to its past glory. There is no dearth of material. The well-crafted stones of the 7th century still lay on the ground and can be put to use for rebuilding the 'city of joy'. The authorities have to stop the unfortunate pilferage of building materials from the site of the temples. These building materials are precious and priceless, they cannot permit such an offhand approach towards the national property.

This was the last entry Kabir made in his diary and he recalled the lines of famous Kashmiri historian Kalhana for King Lalitaditya, "There is no town, village, river or lake where the king did not build a sacred foundation." How true was that! During his reign, he changed the social, cultural and religious fabric of Kashmir. Kabir hoped that Parihasapura would now be entitled to a better name than its current '*kaen shahar*' or 'city of stones'—named so because of the pile of stones and concrete rubble around. He hopes that this landmark architecture once again celebrates the teachings of mutual respect, compassion and love; as was desired by the secular Lalitaditya.

I-16

Pattan Temples

Baramulla

The voluminous *Rajatarangini* mentions that King Sankaravarman, who had ruled over Kashmir during 883–902 AD, had constructed three vast temples at Pattan, now in the district of Baramulla. These three temples were Sankaragaurisvara, Sugandhesa, and Ratnavardhanesa.

Sankaragaurisvara, which is the largest among the three temples, was built in Pattan by the king himself; the second temple was built near Srinagar and was after the queen's name, and Ratnavardhanesa was the third temple and was built by King Sankaravarman's minister. All three temples were dedicated to Shiva. Porches, cell, and a square chamber for the linga is common among all three temples. The designs and patterns are similar to the temple at Mattan. Some of the building material has been taken from the ruins of the Parihasapura temple. While excavating, three water reservoirs and a spring was discovered, which researchers concluded to be the source of the water reservoirs in the complex. Two of the temples are in ruins now but are located at a noticeable location on the national highway.

Kabir was reluctant to carry the voluminous *Rajatarangini* but he had carried the notebook on which he had scribbled a song his grandmother would sing to him:

'Ath Shankargaurisvaras laag pamposhe, sath chum chaine mat roztam roshe
Razan choe guundmoth chae dastaar, yath bhavsagaras detham chev vain taar.'

(I will bedeck the beautiful temple of Shankargaurisvara, Almighty Shankar you are my only hope, so don't remain upset with me. King Sankaravarman has bestowed all the honour upon Lord Shankar, Oh Shankar help me pass through the worldly troubles.)

Kabir's grandmother hailed from the same place Pattan, and this was the folk song most women in the village would sing during any festival or celebration.

In 1847, historian Alexander Cunningham (1814–1893) identified these two temples as the ones mentioned by Kalhana in *Rajatarangini*.

Temple structure

Sugandhesa Temple

I-16a: The lone standing column in the temple.

In the middle of the eastern wall of the peristyle is the entrance to the temple courtyard. The entrance consists of two chambers with a partition wall and a doorway in the middle. It resembles the popular Shankaracharya temple (mentioned later in the book) and the Mattan (located near Pahalgam and an important pilgrimage seat for Kashmiri Pandits) temples in architecture.

A portico in the front leads to a 156 square feet shrine. The main temple stands on a double base. Only one side is open and a trefoil niche is designed on the external side of the other three sides. The niche contains some images, but the flank walls of the lower stair and the frieze of the lower base seem to have been left incomplete. This is evident from the panels which have been blocked out but not carved. There are slots for iron clamps that hold the lower stones of the jambs of the cell. Over time, they have been rusted and corroded but are still extant in some of the mortices.

The cornice of the base of the peristyle is similar to that of the Avantisvami temple. A row of fluted columns is followed by the cells. These cells have a base *in situ*. These are still preserved while the rest are scattered all around the complex.

Sankargaurishvera Temple

This temple was built by King Sankaravarman himself and is only a larger copy of the Sughandesa Temple. It has a large entrance facing the east, with intricate details quite similar to the other temples of Kashmir.

It is an imposing structure but a large area of its grandeur has been taken away due to the conscious decision not to excavate the courtyard. On account of the lack of proper drainage facilities for rainwater, it was advised against any digging for any sort of research. Therefore, the temple plinth, peristyle, and a smaller shrine are still under the ground. The cella has nine circular holes arranged in three rows. The left wall of the portico has a niche divided into two panels, with a probable figure of Shiva-linga and Ganesha. The jambs of the recess on the outside of the temple have half columns which are geometrically designed and have human-headed birds.

Kabir walked out of Sankargaurishvera Temple, looking for the temple built by the minister. Unfortunately, there wasn't much he could find of the Ratnavardhanesa Temple. But there were more interesting things he had discovered. A few metres to the north of these Pattan temples, he bumped into an old *baoli*. It had been recently excavated and the waters were confined in three rectangular reservoirs which were inter-connected. The reservoir in the middle contained a miniature temple, which was constructed originally of three stones. Kabir noticed that the top stone was missing and was open on all sides. The hinges signalled that it must have been originally closed with wooden doors.

In 1857, Cunningham had noticed that the 6 feet by 4 feet chambers of the temple, must have once contained the Shiva-lingas. He had found certain pieces and emblems from the structure being used at Muslim tombs.

Material used

The temple is a complete stone structure. The size of the boulders used is very big. In certain places, there is the use of wood for doors.

What caused the downfall

Alexander Cunningham claims that while the central structure of the temple is completely damaged and ravished, the boundary wall is still intact. A recent study of stones shows that the structure may have come down in the tenth or the eleventh century. The site faced multiple damages, mostly due to earthquakes. The exact dates to some of them have not been confirmed but the one in 1885 had completely ruined the temple complex, and had left the premises in a deplorable plight.

I-16b: The fallen blocks of rock which were once part of the temple.

The structure, Cunningham thinks, was overthrown by Sikandar Butshikan. He believes that both the temples were of such large scale, that the iconoclast must have for sure used gunpowder to bring down the structure. He adds further that Sikandar Butshikan must have had a friendly relationship with Timur-the-lame, who must have gifted this 'villainous saltpetre' to Sikandar.

Current state

Inside the complex there is a lot of loose stuff of things that have been lying since eternity—pieces chipped off, rumbled, or devastated by time, rulers and invaders.

Two bracket capitals with volute ends and carved figures of atlantes support the frieze above, and a huge stone belonging to the cornice of the temple displays rows of *kirtimukhas* (grinning lions' heads), and a carved figure of atlantes support the frieze. There is a stone probably belonging to the partition wall of the entrance. It has two small trefoil niches which show female figures wearing long garlands. Right below the female figures are two rectangular niches, one has an atlante seated between two lion faces and the other are two human heads. At the moment, the temples are not part of any regular religious practice. It does not have pilgrims for spiritual salvation but has tourists, history enthusiasts, and explorers. The temple is in a dilapidated condition and requires serious efforts from the authorities and government. It is heart-wrenching to see the plight of the temple complex, which at the peak of its time must have been buzzing with devotees.

What next

Sculptured stones of this temple with inscriptions in Sharada script have been unearthed from this complex. It has been listed among the 15 important temples for the promotion of tourism in Kashmir. Besides this, the government should do everything possible to restore the lost glory of these temples.

Kabir concluded his day's summary with this note:

> *These shrines were built when the Hindu kings did not have enough wealth to glorify their religion and the prosperity of Hinduism was waning.*

But a curse remains on these temples. They are more popular with the name 'Pattan temples' than with Sankaravarman or Sughandeshwar temples. The curse was that a king who plundered the wealth of Parihaspura to create his town, should not be remembered by his name, rather the town he had created should get the credits.

I-17

Payar Temple

Pulwama

Kabir's research papers told him that there were two rulers by the name of Narendraditya, each in the period of 489–490 AD and 209–222 AD respectively. His research books did not lead him to anything substantial, but it led him to another revelation—Payar Temple.

Payar is a village in the south of Srinagar and is situated 8 km from Pulwama. This unique and beautiful temple is located under a wicker tree, at the foot of the *karewa* (elevated fertile land) and on the opposite side of a rivulet. For many years this temple was popular by the name of Narendraswami Temple built by Narendraditya. Colloquially, later the temple began to be called Payar Temple.

However, the dispute on the dating of the temple continues. Given the architectural style of the temple, it has been concluded that the temple was built around the 11th century.

Temple Structure

The top of the temple is still out of position, yet it is the best-preserved temple of medieval Kashmir times. It is 8 square feet internally and 21 feet in height, which includes the base. The superstructure of the cella has ten stones, it has a single stone on each of the four corners. The sculptured tympanums over the doorways have the other four stones and, two more stones compose the pyramidal roof. The lowest of these is an enormous mass of stone, measuring eight square feet by four feet in height. The torus has a plain moulding in the middle and a filleted torus on the top. Inside, the walls are plain but the roof is hollowed out into a hemispherical. The ornamented wheel at the back can be seen in a good position, but the man ornamented on the forepart of the relief is missing. There is a monster shown here, with a curly mane, an ornamented necklace, and foliated wings. There is a heavily decorated disc at the back. Only four of the five toes in the rear paw of the monster are visible.

I-17a: The small but significant cella.

The roof itself is estimated to be weighing around 7,200 kg. It is divided into two sections, separated by a square-shaped ornamental band, both receding and projecting alternatively. The receding ends are decorated by flowers and the projecting ones are carved into three upright mouldings slightly moulded at the top and surmounted by a straight and horizontal band. The triglyph design for the aesthetic look is particularly remarkable. Gabled niches adorn the blank side of the upper pyramid, which is a replica of the doorways. However, the doorways have a trefoil which is replaced by a semi-circular top and the tympanum has a flower design on it. Melon-like carving has been done on the four pediments and the apex of the roof. Of the four pediments, two are out of shape and two are still in shape. A single flight of stairs on the east side leads to the sanctum. The doorways are rectangular and are surmounted by a trefoil arch, which is in turn enclosed by a pediment. The pilaster on which these pediments rest is adorned by a pair of geese with long foliate tails and the pilaster from which the trefoil arches springs are surmounted by recumbent bull capitals. The bulls have scarves tied to their humps.

The eastern trefoil has Shiva seated crossed-legged under a canopy of an overhanging tree, surmounted by two votaries seated with their legs hanging down. On the northern side is the Bhairav form of Shiva; one can see an elephant trunk in the background. The scene depicted here is of Bhairav pursuing a human being, who turns towards him in an attitude of supplication. On the western side is the six-armed manifestation of a dancing Shiva. The upper two arms are seen holding a scarf, the middle two hands are gesticulating, the lowest left-hand holds a flower, and the right-hand holds the trident. In the same scene, a group of musicians is playing the *veena*. On the southern end is seen a three-headed, crossed-legged Shiva who is seated on a wicker-work pedestal. He is only two-armed here and is seen wearing the sacred Brahmanical thread. Around his head is the *Yaksha*. On his left lower corner is a female figure, who probably is Parvati, his consort. There are three other female figures, but they all look to be emaciated, hence researchers assume them to be ascetics. The corner pilaster is crowned by very beautiful floral capitals.

The sculptures over the doorways have been defaced but represent Brahma, Vishnu, Shiva, and Goddess Durga.

In comparison to the aesthetically done architecture of the temple, the doorways have been coarsely executed. The temple is dedicated to Vishnu as the Sun God or Surya. Probably that is the reason why inside the cupola, each corner is illuminated to represent the Sun. At each corner of the square, the space intervening between the angle and the line of the circle is filled by celestial carved attendants who seem to be beautifully placed. A Shiva-linga can still be seen inside the cella.

The Shiva carving shown seated on a wicker base is smeared with vermillion. On close-ups, most carvings have been worn off, and the stone is jagged at many places, yet from a distance, the temple is an architectural marvel.

All around urbanization has added a modern dynamic to the complex. Many locals residing around are the silent keepers of the temple. Their tall houses visually appear to be guarding the temple from all four sides.

Material used

Granite stone has been used in the construction of the temple.

I-17b: Human figure with stretched arms as part of the ceiling design.

What caused the downfall

The temple has been weathered away by time and nature. It is believed by certain researchers that the Pathans (tribe from northwest plains) had attempted to destroy the temple, and the partially demolished roof of the temple was caused by that attack. However, they soon concluded that the Payar Temple was not of much interest to the Pathans and hence they left it midway.

It is also assumed that an earthquake may have possibly caused some harm to the structure.

Current state

The temple is nestled inside a beautiful green patch. Even from a distance its beauty and artistic carvings are distinct. The majestic Chinars add a captivating backdrop to the temple. The complex is guarded with a boundary wall and inside are pitched the ASI information boards. The recently constructed main gate remains locked on most occasions and often a guard is seen marching around the place.

What next

The temple has been classified as a 'Monument of national importance' by the ASI, but it certainly is a complex which is left to the apathy of times. It is forlorn and lost and has no mention in any of the 'must-visit' places in Kashmir.

Besides the historical relevance of the site, the complex has tremendous importance for the followers of Hinduism.

Perhaps promoting the cultural relevance of the Payar Temple, hosting small events, educating about the architectural style, the stone carving, etc. can be a huge source of revenue for the State.

Kabir in his notes couldn't conclude which Narendraditya was the actual king to commission the Payar Temple, but he certainly knew that the temple was a jewel in stone, irrespective of who had built it.

I-18
Sharda Temple
Pakistan Occupied Kashmir

Visiting this temple wasn't easy. Kabir had to seek the permission of the central as well as the state government to visit this temple. The grand Sharda temple is in the Pakistan Occupied Kashmir (POK) area, close to the Line of Control. It is 63 km from Srinagar. Perched in the picturesque Neelum Valley, Sharda Peeth is considered to be the *kul-devi* (deity of a clan/family) of the Kashmiri Pandits. Sharda is the Kashmiri name for the Goddess of wisdom, Saraswati. The Goddess is said to resemble a swan, who is seen carrying glittering gold in her hand.

I-18a: File picture of a Kashmiri Hindu standing at the old structure of the temple.

Sharda Peeth, meaning the 'place of knowledge', has in ancient times been the epicentre of intellectual discussions and debate. Scholars from China, Tibet, Cambodia, Afghanistan, and Bhutan travelled to this *peeth* for the exchange of knowledge. It was constructed even before the centres of learning at Nalanda and Taxila were set up. Spiritual Guru Shankaracharya, Jain scholar Hem Chandra, poet-historian Bilhana, and historian Jonaraja visited Sharda Peeth in 1422 (Kashmir was under the rule of Zain-ul-Abdin during this period). Buddhist translator Vairotsana (who was believed to be a reincarnation of a Kashmiri Pandit), also visited this centre of learning. History, logic, vedic learning, science, religion, and geography were some of the subjects of discourse and discussion at Sharda Peeth. Adi Guru Shankaracharya had composed 'Panchastavi', a prayer in praise of Goddess Sharda at this *tirtha*.

According to the puranic story, when the body of Goddess Sati was cut into 51 pieces, her right hand had fallen at Sharda Peeth, therefore this place has immense relevance as a Shaktipeeth amongst Hindu devotees.

Devotees from Kashmir even perform the rituals for their departed forefathers at the *sangam* of the holy rivers of Sindhu and Madhumati.

Temple Structure

Neelum river, which flows through the valley and is a custodian of many stories, was called Krishan-Ganga in ancient times. Next to this gurgling and frothy river is the village of Sardi which is located to the west of the district Kupwara. In the surrounding is the breath-taking Nanga Parbat.

Before the partition of India, this was a regular place of *tirtha* for Kashmiri Hindus. But after the partition and invasion of Kashmir by the Pakistani forces, the Hindus of the valley couldn't visit the *peeth*.

The temple was first found around 200 BC during the reign of Ashoka. This base structure was later built upon by King Lalitaditya during his reign.

A flight of ancient steps from outside the premises leads the visitor to the temple complex. The steps are constructed out of massive rectangular stones. A railing to support pedestrians has been the recent modern addition to it.

At the landing, a large shrine catches the imagination of the visitor. At the prime of its existence, the temple compound was forfeited by an 11 feet wall. From the remnants, it can be seen that it was constructed out of big boulders which weren't easy to ferry. Like most other temples of Kashmir, the big stones have neatly been held together with a good mix of lime plaster.

The large temple structure is in the middle of the compound. A flight of a further few steps lead the visitor to the top of the terrace. These steps aren't in shape and are deceptive at certain places. Weather and human obstruction have left the temple in a dilapidated condition. These steps are 4 feet wide and lead to the veranda on which the door of the main temple opens. This veranda is supported by two pillars and is 4 feet wide. There may have been some intricate engraving and designs inscribed on these structures, but nothing is visible now, not even any faint outlines.

The main temple structure stands on a plinth which is 24 feet in length and is at a height of 5 feet from the ground. The enclosure inside is approximately 13 square feet in area. The arches of the temple are about 8 feet. Right in the *garba* (centre) of the temple is a stone slab, which is 7 feet in length and 6 feet in width. The massive slab is half a foot in width. Hindus believe that there is a *nag* under this slab, but the slab hasn't been moved in centuries. *Shri Chakra* is inscribed on the top of this stone slab. *Shri Chakra* represents a circular wheel of life, depicted through one basic central point that represents the core of the universe. Around this, there are 3 circles, 4 gates to enter, and 43 triangles showing the corners of the *Shri Chakra* and the cosmic form of Mahadevi. With time, these impressions have become light and not recognizable.

There are some inscriptions in Sharada script on some of the stone tiles, and an impression of Shiva's Trishul can be inferred. To the west of the temple is a fort-like structure called Sirhasila Castle, which is sadly in ruins now. In ancient times, this fort was encircled by Krishnaganag, Madhumati and Muktasri rivers.

I-18b: The worn-out outer wall of the temple with arched pattern.

Between 1846–56, during the Dogra rule, King Gulab Singh constructed a fort near the temple, to secure the safety of the visiting devotees. He had even renovated some parts of the temple.

Chinese travellers stayed at this temple for many years. Poet-historian Kalhana mentions that during the rule of the liberal King Lalitaditya, the king of Bengal took a pilgrimage to Sharda Peeth.

As Kabir was researching, the locals at POK told him that there is another Sharda *peeth* at Yachkoot near Badgam in Srinagar. It is housed inside a hollow Chinar tree, which is part of a groove of five to six Chinar trees.

Material used

The entire temple is constructed out of grey limestone boulders. Their size is massive and their transportation to this point of elevation is astonishing.

What caused the downfall

Sharda Peeth was the most revered and holiest place for Hindus. During the Hindu rule, the temple was in a spic and span condition, but later during the Mughal and Pathan rule, the upper Krishanganga area was completely neglected and politically disturbed. The temple got ignored then. Fortunately, during the Dogra rule, conditions at the temple improved marginally, but they worsened after the partition in 1947.

Natural calamities and the brutal miseries of time have cast their shadow upon the temple structure. The temple site had also witnessed multiple earthquakes. One of the earthquakes had partially damaged the temple stairs.

The site suffered another earthquake in 2005, but no restoration was initiated and it stands as it is.

Current state

Quoting Abu-i-Fazal from his book, *Ain-i-Akbari* from the 16th century, "...on the banks of river Madhumati, is a stone temple, dedicated to Goddess Durga and regarded with great veneration. On every eight days of the bright moon, it begins to shake and produces the most extraordinary effect..." He even quoted that there was evidence of statues of gold and silver at this shrine.

In 1030, historian Al-Baruni visited Sharda Peeth and mentioned a wooden idol of Goddess Sharda at the temple complex.

As per *Martand Mahatmaya*, sage Shandilya, who meditated in the Sharda-*van*, was blessed to receive the vision of Goddess Sharda. As instructed by the Goddess, he followed her through different hillocks and *nags*, until she finally revealed herself to the sage at the Sharda sacred spot and rewarded his austerities by inviting him to Her residence Sirhasila. Poet-historian Kalhana mentions about Sharda temple and its location in *Rajatarangini*.

Another puranic story narrates that after the *Sagar Manthan*, the leftover nectar along with the *Kalash* was taken away by the six-armed Goddess Sharda. She got that nectar in the *Kalash* straight to a place called Shardi and hid it under a stone slab. It is believed that the nectar she carried along was of wisdom and knowledge, and is under the same stone slab, therefore warranting reverence.

The temple complex is not under the control of the Indian Union. Unfortunately, it is under the illegitimate governance of an Islamic-majority nation. The temple is at no one's mercy. There is no association or body to look after it.

In 1947, the presiding pandit of the temple, Swami Nandlalji Maharaja was forced to flee from the temple. The hassled pandit is said to have brought some idols from the temple. He lugged these stone idols over horses, across to Kashmir. These idols were then preserved in the temples of Kupwara and Devibal at Baramulla in Kashmir.

The 1947–48 partition and subsequent wars between India and Pakistan further worsened the condition of the temple. Fear and threat played on the innocent minds of the Kashmiri Pandits and they never went back on any holy pilgrimage to Sharda Peeth. Wild grass has grown on the top of the boundary wall. The entire sanctum is disfigured and discoloured. Even the main sanctum has wild in-grown vegetation in the crevices of the walls. There is a film of dead and dry moss across the structure. There is an information board about the temple, which is written in Urdu and is signed by the Archaeological Department of Pakistan. The most revered place of Hindu minorities of the Kashmir valley is in dire need of restoration and attention.

What next

In 2019, the central government in collaboration with the then-Pakistan government initiated the Kartarpur Sahib corridor. It is a visa-free, religious corridor between the Dera Baba Nanak in Gurdaspur, Punjab, India, and Gurudwara Darbar Sahib near Lahore, Pakistan. Both are revered places for the Sikh community.

Inspired by this initiative of the government, the Save Sharda Committee Kashmir, lead by Ravinder Pandita, took up the cause of saving the crumbling and deplorable Sharda temple. They were inspired by the initiation of the opening of the Uri, Rawalkot, and Poonch Corridors by the neighbouring countries. The committee nursed some hopes of a similar Sharda corridor, through which Hindus can visit their most revered *peeth*.

Save Sharda Committee Kashmir is one such organization that is working relentlessly for access to be granted to the Hindu community. They have requested amendments in the visa rules and sought access to the annual Sharda pilgrimage, which had been a routine event during ancient times in Kashmir. A memo has also been presented for the construction of a Sharda University.

Even the residents of POK address the temple shrine with a lot of respect and call her Mai Sharada. They wish for their Hindu brethren to visit the temple and desire the place to resonate with prayers and spiritual energy like it used to many centuries ago.

During a civil society exchange, the natives of POK bedecked the inner sanctum with the photo of Goddess Sharda and offered some flowers to her on behalf of her devotees from Kashmir. Later, the residents of POK sent these flowers and some mud from the pious land of Sharda Peeth to the members of Save Sharda Committee Kashmir.

Kabir's concluding visit to Sharda Peeth was the turning point of his life. For 30 years his grandmother's *gurumantra* was his first 'thought of the day'. The mantra goes like:

Namestey Sharada Devi Kashmira-Pura-Vasini, Tvamaham Prarthaye Nityam Vidya-Danam Che Dehi Mey

(Salutations to you, O Sharada, O Goddess, the one who resides in Kashmir. I pray to you daily, please give me the charity of knowledge).

And that day he was standing on the pious land of Goddess Sharda mumbling these divine words.

I-19
Vijeshwara Temple
Anantnag

"Where one is free from worries, agony, and pain where it is easy to control oneself and one's ambitions, where peace of mind and spiritual solace can be achieved, where spiritually elevated persons remain in un-interrupted meditation, in that place which is called Vijeshwara, the Devtas aspire to be born."

(From *Sahatya Prakash*[1])

Vijeshwara also known as Bijbehara, is in Anantnag district, next to the river Jhelum or Vitasta. It is a town of immense religious significance since ancient times.

Amongst all the temples visited so far, Vijeshwara temple has been the most mysterious and cryptic one experienced by Kabir. This place left Kabir more mesmerized not by the look of the remnants but by

---

[1] Acharya Abhinavagupt, the great philosopher, mystic, exegete, theologian; whose work has influenced a large part of the Kashmiri thoughts on life and religion is believed to have written this book. However, due to unfortunate cultural and religious wars which impaired the routines of the naïve Kashmiris, this script and a lot of his work were destroyed and wiped out. The aforementioned phrase has been kept alive by the Kashmiri Pandit community through the word of mouth. Therefore, a physical copy of the lost manuscript cannot be presented. However, the above mentioned line has been duly verified from scholars and authors in the Kashmiri Pandit community.

the many folklores that he absorbed from the locals of Bijbehara. He couldn't cover so many voices in a single day. He had to pay multiple visits to listen, understand and engage with the various locals.

He had been sitting under an old Chinar tree for the longest time, perhaps absorbing the place. Just about then an old lady passed by and warmed up to him, "Did you know that this is the oldest Chinar in the entire Kashmir valley and was planted by the Mughal Emperor himself?"

Kabir was startled to know this. "Do you live here, Maeji?" he asked.

And the old lady blurted out like a cloudburst. "Son, you will have to spend an entire lifetime to know about Bijbehara and the enlightened souls that lived here, ages ago. You are an outsider with limited time, so I can only share the tip of this fountainhead of wisdom. This city was called the 'City of Sanskrit'. River Vitasta passes through two ancient *tirthas,* named Vijeshwara and Cakardhara. Vijeshwara was a city of learning and in early times there was a university that attracted scholars from all around the world to indulge themselves in the ocean of knowledge. My son, the tower of the temple at Vijeshwara was believed to be 11 feet tall. During sunrise, the shadow of the tower would fall on Vodur at Mattan, and at sunset, the shadow would fall on the premises of the Martand temple. Vijeshwara emerged as the greatest place of learning and knowledge over the period. Philosophy, medicine, literature, astronomy, astrology, sculpturing, painting, Hindu and Buddhist scriptures research papers, and music, were some of the subjects being taught here to students coming from all over the world. It was here at Vijeshwara or Bijbehara that Pandit Kalhana completed his *Rajatarangini*, Khem-Raj wrote *Shiv-sidhant* and Acharya Somdev wrote *Katha Sarit Sagar* and *Vaitaal Pachisi*."

She stopped to catch her breath and continued, "What more do you wish to know about this land of the sacred Vijeshwara Kshetra?

I-19a: The pit with sculptured tiles of Gods and Goddesses.

I am not a Hindu, but I know when Rishi Kashyap was setting up the Kashmir valley for people, he had commissioned the construction of a replica of the famous Harishchandra Ghat of Varanasi (one of the pilgrimages in India) at this spiritual place. It is located next to the Shiva temple on the southern end, look over there."

She left immediately after her monologue leaving behind an awestruck Kabir. It seemed as though she was sent with a purpose. Kabir was even more perplexed and confused than before. Kabir followed her but she was too fast for her age. She vanished in the labyrinths of the village streets.

According to Kalhana's *Rajatarangini*, this town was founded by King Vijayanand, King Gopaladeva's son around the 6th century. But the existence of two earlier temples built by Ashoka, named Ashokavara, indicates that Ashoka had visited the site even before Vijayanand. Later, during Vijayanand's reign, he added on and built further to the structure already built by King Ashoka. Another finding which was later corroborated by Aurel Stein, mentions that King Ashoka had replaced the old stuccoed enclosure of the temple with one of the stones. But these temples so often mentioned by Kalhana have disappeared completely. Historian Aurel Stein says, "It is possible that a temple so much frequented had undergone more than one restoration in the course of the fifteen centuries which passed between the time of Ashoka and the end of Hindu reign in Kashmir."

Temple Structure

There is nothing left of the original structure of the massive temple. Not a single concrete temple or structure of any ancient form is to be seen. On the contrary, there are numerous ruins and remains of the erstwhile temple, which can be spotted all across the town of Bijbehara. A lot of stuff from here was moved to the SPS Museum in 1898 by Captain Godfrey.

Next to Vitasta, there is a pit that has the most beautifully carved stone idols and tiles. Some of them have been pasted inside the low-height wall of the pit. It has a Ganesh idol, Shiva riding the loyal Nandi, a Shiva-linga, deity figures, the statue of a lion, and many other such artefacts.

Using the material from the demolished temple, Maharaja Gulab Singh and Maharaja Ranbir Singh reconstructed the present-day Harishchandra *ghat*. During the rule of Raja Pratap Singh, the new and current Vijeshwara temple was erected, hence preserving the remaining idols and sculptures. There are four small temples of Vishnu on Garuda, two Nandis; one with the Shiva-linga and a separate temple for a group of small Shiva-lingas, small tiles of Bhairav, and village deity Ananeshwar. The temple was restored phenomenally during the Dogra reign.

I-19b: Lone sculpture of Nandi.

Material used

The ruins point at the use of granite stone.

What caused the downfall

For destroyer Sikandar Butshikan, Vijeshwara was a temple site that had to be plundered at all costs. Certain researchers contest that when Sikandar arrived at

Vijeshwara, he was clueless on how to bring the 11 feet tall structure down. Locals of Vijeshwara concur with this and add that there were cryptic inscriptions written on the stone slabs of the temple. Nobody could decipher these codes. Sikander Butshikan kept prize money for anyone who could read the codes and eventually bring the structure down. In the sleepy village, a potter volunteered and moved a certain slab or a connector in the entire structure and got the concrete down. It was later understood that the coded words, loosely translated here meant—anyone with a pure and pious soul and who has never thought, uttered, or enacted any evil will know the secret to the structure.

Amongst the many Shiva-lingas at the site, most have been destroyed by Sikander Butshikan.

Another reason cited is that in 1081 AD, King Ananta was visiting Vijeshwara on a pilgrimage, and at that time the temple was burnt down in a general conflagration caused by his son Kalasha.

Current state

One can see many relics from the temple lying all around the vicinity of the erstwhile temple. Ruins can also be spotted in and around the entire town of Bijbehara, which probably belonged to the temple. Some ruins can be found in and around the Bade Masjid. Outside the Ratan Haji mosque, a stone receptacle for temple offerings is found. It even has a pillar inside it.

The temple site is also a crude reminder of the excavated Burzahom prehistoric settlement, which inhabited this region around 3000 and 1000 BC.

Small temple enclosures and walls can be spotted which are painted in brick red colour. This is the result of the conservation work done under the Dogra rule.

What next

Delegation of Vijeshwar Devasthan Trust (Regd) Tehsil Bijbehara submitted a memorandum to Deputy Commissioner Anantnag, requesting for taking up of reconstruction and renovation of Pracheen Amarnath Cave Shrine Thajiwara Bijbehara and Vijeshwara Temple Bijbehara through Department of Archaeology and culture.

There is a Herculean task to be done in restoring the past glory of this site. The list of things to be accomplished is endless:

Restore research work—The government should allocate financial and intellectual funds so that scholars can visit for research work and reinstate the lost glory of the place.

Generate awareness—Put the temple site on the heritage map of India. It is not only an important historical location but even a cultural one.

Attract tourists—The authorities should host events like light and sound shows or literary or cultural exchange programs.

On Kabir's concluding day at Vijeshwara also called by the new generation of Srinagar as the 'Pit temple', Maeji appeared again. This time she wore a deep almond-coloured *pheran* and a floral printed scarf, which covered her head and both ears. In her mystical way, she asked him, "Son, are you leaving today?"

Kabir shuddered at the query. *How did she get to know that I was leaving?*

"God be with you. Before you leave do touch that stone, which weighs 80 kg, looks like a conch shell, and is a mystical stone that can only be lifted when 11 people gather together and chant loudly *kah-kah-kah* (meaning number 11 in Kashmiri). Using only their index finger, magically they can lift it. These are the strange ways of the Almighty! In Him, we all believe and with unity, we all must live," saying so Maeji disappeared again.

Kabir's last day at Vijeshwaraa was truly other-worldly.

Part II

Ancient Temples
(Completely decimated and lost)

After an intensive field research, Kabir had decided to spend the remaining couple of weeks with his father in Shimla. His tickets were arranged by Shakeel, who was visiting his family on a holiday.

"I know, you want to go home, but spend a few more days here, we can do a trek to the great lakes of Kashmir. I have a friend who can make the arrangements," implored Shakeel.

It was an interesting proposition and Kabir had heard a lot about the six famous lakes of Kashmir—Vishansar lake, Gangbal lake, Krishansar lake, Nundkol lake, Satsar lake and the Gadsar lake. His grandmother had visited the Gangbal lake when she was just married to his grandfather. She fondly remembered her first pilgrimage trip with her husband to Harmukh Ganga.

"You know, Shakeel, this mention about the great lakes of Kashmir reminds me about the song my grandmother would often sing. For the longest time I thought it was a love song, but after this trip to the ancient and revered temples of Kashmir, I now understand the subtle philosophical and spiritual meaning to the song. There is deep meaning in every word of the song as though Goddess Parvati is waiting for Shiva to come down from the Harmukh mountain range and resolve the mysteries of the world. The song goes like this:

Harmokh bartal praraey madaano,
Yee daphum tee laagayoo,

Poosh daphem gulaab,
Laagai madaano, Yee daphum tee laagayoo,

Shaeyri daphem gulaab,
Laagai madaano, Yee daphum tee laagayo,

Phambas te naaras myul goom,
Wallah meh czei path dil goom,
Be'no ye dooryer cshalaai madaano,
Yee daphum tee laagayo,

Kongas karmei chamayee,
Maenz hoo laagai naman,
Mushtaq goham kaman madano,
Yee daphum tee laagayo.

I will wait for you at the gate of Hurmukh, oh! my love,
Whatever you will ask for I will provide you,

If you will ask for a flower, I will provide you a rose
Whatever you will ask for I will provide you,

Cotton and fire are now one,
Oh God! My heart is stuck on you,

I can't bear this distance anymore, oh! my love,
Whatever you ask for I will do that for you,

I have put you in the fields of saffron,
I will fill your nails with henna,
Yearning for whom my love,
Whatever you will ask for I will do that for you."

Kabir stopped mid-way and realized that Shakeel's father was also humming the song. Both choked up with an overwhelming rush of emotions and hugged each other.

Shakeel's father spoke with moist eyes, "Kabir, you have been working so hard to connect with your roots and to tell the world about the wonder Kashmir is. But as your well wisher, I suggest if you add a few more destinations to your exploration, your University work will be more exhaustive and comprehensive."

Shakeel's father took a large sip of the pink tea called *sheerchai*, along with thick layer of white cream sitting on the top of the cup. He spoke in between chewing the *nankhatai* and rolling the greasy white cream in his mouth, "Kabir, here have a look at these places. They are the names of the ancient monuments and temples which have been destroyed and decimated. You may find them of interest. This list was handed over to me by an ex-colleague, who had briefly worked with the ASI and was quite impressed by the nature of your work."

Kabir willingly took that paper and since the names were written in Urdu, he requested Shakeel's father to read them out. The list, Kabir realized, was long and he could not leave for Shimla without visiting those places. He stayed back for not only his research but for the promise he had made to his grandmother.

II-20

Andarkot

A few kilometres from Shadipur, which is at the confluence point of rivers Vitasta and Sindhu (modern names are Jhelum and Sindh), is the village of Andarkot. It was the ancient capital of King Jayapida and was popular by the name Jayapura. The ruins of an ancient temple can be seen in the region. They are scattered all across and must have been built during the rule of King Jayapida.

Andarkot is the new name of Jayapura and is located near the village of Sumbal. There isn't much that is left of the Buddhist *viharas* and Hindu temples, which were built in the 7th or the 8th century. There is a heap of big boulders and stones left of the Hindu Keshava temple. Further around, a couple of sculptured reliefs on two faces of the pilaster of the stairs can be seen. The relief on the stairs depicts a four-armed Vishnu seated on a *lalitasana* (cushioned seat). His left foot rests on a footstool. His upper right hand holds a mace and his lower left hand are placed in *abhaymudra* (pose of granting immunity from fear). On the left side is a female attendant standing. Vishnu is heavily ornamented and wears the *mandarmala*. Under his throne are an atlante and some other indistinct figures. Vishnu is shown seated along with his two consorts displayed on the relief of the front panel.

Besides this, Andarkot has other historical significance too. This was the spot where the last Hindu ruler, Queen

Kota Rani surrendered to her rebellious servant Shah Mir on a certain stipulation which he did not even fulfil later.

Another interesting information about Andarkot is that when it was chosen to be the capital city, the complete area was in the midst of a marshy land. Cleaning and clearing up this was a Herculean task. Later during the 12th century, the time when Kalhana wrote *Rajatarangini*, it was believed that King Jayapida must have employed *rakshasas* or demons from his friend King Vibhishana of Ceylon to accomplish this colossal job.

II-21
Amritabhavana

Amritaprabha, Queen of Meghavahana (12–46 AD), had built a temple called Amritabhavana. It is located towards the east of Vichar *nag*. The temple is in complete ruins now. No visible standing structure or any relics can be spotted, but locals say that if the authorities dig the earth, they will discover many parts of the lost temple.

II-22
Amburher

On the way towards the Sindh valley from Srinagar city, there is an ancient village called Amburher. Queen Suryamati (1028–1086 AD) had found two religious centres here. Ruins of this can be seen used in the construction of a *ziarat* of Saint Farukhzad Sahib, which is located in the same vicinity.

II-23

Bhimakeshava

About three kilometres to the north of Mattan on the Srinagar-Pahalgam highway is a Vishnu temple which is located on the left of the Lidder River. This Bhimakeshava temple is in the village of Bumazav. The uppermost stone of the ceiling is carved into a full-blown lotus. The pyramidal roof is with two tiers. Its interior is eight square feet and is open on all sides.

In design, it is similar to Pandrethan. Queen Didda built this temple in memory of her father King Bhima Shahi. She had built numerous shrines of Vishnu. Amongst them was one in the memory of her deceased son, her father, and herself. This *matha* is next to river Jhelum in SafaKadal in the Srinagar city

II-24

Firozpur-Drang

Firozpur is a small village situated near Tangmarg, at the point where the Firozpor *nalla*, opens up into the ground. The latter part of the name Drang (popular during the pre-Muslim times), means 'frontier watch station', which was established during the Karkota reign for the purpose of collection of duties and taxes.

This village has the ruins of a small temple, which is probably surrounded by a peristyle. Only a double-chambered door is visible, while the rest of the temple is under the thick foliage of vegetation. Trees and ingrowth have ruined the temple. The unchecked growth of walnut trees has taken root in the masonry. The temple faces the northeast and the roof has fallen inside completely. The ceiling and the external style of the temple seem to be of the Narasthan style. Slight projection on the corner pilasters and the trefoil recesses on the sides are smaller than the arch of the portico; which is again like Narasthan. The inner chamber area is 11 square feet. Large boulders have covered up much of the floor, hence making it difficult to ascertain the sculpture of the presiding deity.

The portico was surmounted by a trefoil arch and a pediment of the usual type. The temple stands on a base surmounted by a cyma recta moulding. A plain side wall at the sideways of the steps lead to the temple. The gateway is 15 feet tall.

Ascending, there is a beautiful piece of land that is in the midst of a dense forest, from where scanty remains of the base of the small temple are visible. Nothing much is known about the structure, but the natives believe that there had been another structure in the complex. Maybe they are now hidden under the earth.

II-25
Garur

Near the north-eastern side of Wular lake lies the village of Garur. It houses a small temple with the dimensions of 7 feet 3 inches high from the basement to the cornice and internally measures 16 square feet. The base is underground and the roof has disappeared. The ceiling is built of overlapping stones. A flight of steps that go down to the spring, which was near the temple, is missing. Even the roof of the temple must have been in pediment design. The absence of an external trefoil niche is remarkable. There is a pointed niche in each of these walls that contain a sculptured relief. On the back of these is a three-headed Shiva. There are two other figures but nothing can be confirmed about them with certainty.

II-26

Gupkar Temple

The famous Gupkar Road of Srinagar has many ancient temples, which were constructed by King Gopaladitya. On the roadside, a large Shiva-linga, which is ten feet in diameter can be seen lying scattered. It had been broken and the pieces have been used for other building purposes. Even large carved slabs from here have been used to build *ziarats* at places around.

II-27

Gupt Ganga

Ishbar, a popular place in Srinagar city, was called Ishvar in olden times. A sacred spring is the main attraction of the place. A square mound measuring an area of 30 square feet and about three feet in height is located next to the spring. A large pile of temple ruins can be seen lying at the site. Local *purohits* believe that this mound was the site for the temple built by King Sandhiman, and their statement concurs with the researchers and academicians too. Numerous ancient buildings are found around the area. This has been further mentioned by Kalhana, where he points out to the erection of various temples at the site of Sureshvari-kshetra by Avantivarman's minister named Shura (856–883 AD).

II-28
Khonmuh

Khonamusa is the ancient name for the modern Khonmuh. This is also the birthplace of Bilahan, the famous poet from Kashmir, who lived during the reign of King Kalasha (1036–89 AD).

Khonmuh contains the ruins of an ancient temple next to a tank. This ancient temple is a cave shrine of Lord Shiva located atop a hill. A Shiva-linga is placed inside the temple. During peaceful times, the locals would visit the temple during *Shravan Poornima*. Unfortunately, the Shiva-linga has been slayed and lies on the side of the ground. In the good old days, this was also a bustling venue for the start of the Amarnath Yatra. Nowadays, the temple wears a deserted look.

II-29
Khrew

To the south of Khonmuh is the village of Khrew. The ancient name for this place is Khanduvi. At this place lies the shrine of Goddess Jwala. There is a monolithic temple of stone (miniature one). However, there isn't much known about the antiquity of this temple site.

II-30

Kuil

Between Avantipura and Payar there is a miniature temple built out of a single stone. The interior of the temple is a cube of 15 inches and the centre of the roof is doomed out into a dome. The walls are five inches thick and there is only one entrance. Doorways on three sides are closed with pediments similar to the entrance, which is in trefoil. The pediment is absolute. On either side of the vestibule, the figure of a deity is carved into bold relief on the panel contained within a trefoil arched access. The basement and upper division of the roof are not found. At the base, the plinth is seven inches high and approximately 12 inches wide. Small columns of eight inches in diameter are found in the structure. In appearance, the temple looks similar to the Payar and the Pandrethan temples.

The wall on the three sides has an arched blank recess. On the wall on the northern side is a small square postern measuring around 3 feet by 5 feet. A similar one on the west side seems to be leading to the south corner of the temple. A small arched window throws light inside the chamber. Projecting into the chamber from the southern wall is a small cella about 5 square feet with a pyramidal roof. Kuil is imposing and more detailed than Payar and Pandrethan.

Each side is about 15 feet in height. The porch on the west side projects more than 3 feet from the wall. The inner entrance is a square gateway of 6 by 3 feet in height and width. Both this and the middle gateway in the north have been fitted with stone doors. The inner chamber is about 8 feet in the square. On the south side of the entrance is a small arched recess but the rest of the walls are blank. The flooring is of stone.

II-31

Narpristan

This temple is amongst the first few ancient temples of Srinagar. Popular as Narendra-Swamin, this temple was built by King Lakhana-Narendraditya (209–222 AD). It is located between Habba Kadal and Fateh Kadal. It has now been converted into a *ziarat* now and is called Narpristan.

II-32

Naranthal

Three kilometres away from Baramulla on the Muzaffarabad Road, is the ancient temple of Naranthal. It has a mention in the *Nilamata Purana* as well. The temple has an area of 256 square feet. It has plain walls and a 3 feet wide doorway. It stands in a small tank and has an arched entrance from the east. The superstructure is above the ground and is made of slate stones. The interior area is 7 square feet and the height is 10 feet. The roof has a circular mortice in the centre, which was originally built to hold the finial. The circular mortice in the centre crowned the apex of the pyramid. The second layer is also formed of a single slate stone. This temple is probably from the 12th century.

II-33
Pampur

King Padma had found Pampur in the 9th century. Pampur is about 4 miles southwest of Khrew. Although King Padma was born in a spirit distiller's house, he rose to become an important and all-powerful ruler of Kashmir. He was the maternal uncle to puppet-king, Chipatta-Jayapida (802–14 AD). He consecrated the temple of Padmasvami-Vishnu at Pampur (Pampur is referred to as Padmapura in *Rajatarangini*). Aurel Stein mentions in his book that the remains of this ancient cella can now be seen scattered near the shrine of Mir-Mohammad Hamadani. Two of its fluted columns, ornamented slabs, and other carved stones are part of this shrine now. There is another *ziarat* close to this temple, and shows the use of fine and ancient remains of the temple structure.

II-34
Raneshvara

In the south of Vichar *nag* is the temple of Raneshvara, built by King Ranaditya (223 AD). The ruins of this structure can be seen at the Madin Sahib mosque.

II-35
Sadhbhavna Shri

Pravarsena II, the king of Kashmir had built a temple, which can now be located a few kilometres away from

Kaen Kadal. This is located to the west of Jama Masjid. Parts of the temple have been used in the building of a *ziarat* of Pir Haji Muhammad. Of the remnants, one can see a temple pillar outside the masjid. Sultan Qutb-ud-din was buried at the same spot.

II-36
Skanda-Bhavana

Skanda Gupta, minister in the royal court of King Yudhistra II (170–209 AD), had constructed a temple. The relics of this structure can now be located near Nawa Kadal. The temple being in ruins now is called Khanda Bhavana. Some of the building material has been used for a *ziarat* of Pir Muhammad Basur.

Another ancient temple that was constructed by Pravarsena can be seen in ruins now. They are called as Lauki-Shri and the *ghat* of the temple is still called *Lokhi Yarbal.*

II-37
Siligram

On the Anantnag-Pahalgam highway there is a temple named Siligram. This Shiva temple is the rarest in entire India. The Shiva-linga has a thousand eyes on its body and has the most beautiful presentation. As per Kalhana, this temple was an important stopover for devotees going to Amarnath. It was also popularly known as the Sahastramukha temple. After the exodus of Kashmiri Pandits from the valley, this temple and the Shiva-linga were vandalized and broken into pieces. The broken structure still lies there.

II-38
Tapar

Approximately 12 kilometres from Baramulla towards Srinagar is a village called Tapar. It houses the ruins of an ancient temple built by Narendraprabha, Queen of Pratapaditya II, who had reigned from 634 to 684 AD. The temple was called Narendreshvara. Sikandar, the iconoclast, and Zain-ul-Abidin (1420–70 AD) ruined the temple and used the stones in the construction of the bridge from Naidkhai to Sopore.

II-39
Tarapida Temple

Towards the east of Jama Masjid is the famous Tarapida Temple built by King Tarapida (696–670 AD). This site is considered sacred even by Buddhists. The ancient name given to this temple by the people from Ladakh is Tsitsung Tsublak Kang. However, the main deity of the temple is still unknown.

II-40
Tribhuvan Swamin

Going further down on the left of the river Jhelum near the 6th bridge (Srinagar has a total of 7 significant bridges running across various points in the city) is another temple ruin, which was built by King Chandrapida (687–698 AD). The temple was built of stone and was popular by the name Tribhuvwithaswamin. A Muslim saint named Thug Baba Sahib is buried close to this site and therefore the place is now also popular by the name of Thug Baba Sahib.

II-41
Thajuvur Temple

On way to Pahalgam, towards the east of Bijbehara a beautiful cave is situated at the descent of a plateau. Goddess Parvati is said to have meditated in this cave for 12 years and therefore this cave has high spiritual importance for the residing Hindus of the valley. This cave is the abode of Shiva and Parvati. It was an important point of halt for pilmgrims travelling to the holy cave of Amarnath, and hence gets the name 'Swami Amarnath Thajuvur'. Devotees who are unable to visit Amarnath cave because of its tough terrain, can pray to Lord Shiva at Thajuvur cave temple. Unfortuantely, like most other revered places, even this cave temple wasn't spared. Post 1990, the entire 25 acres of land has been illegally occupied and the infrastructure was demolished. Since then entire developmental work of Thajuvur Managing Committee has come to a standstill.

II-42
Ushkar-Baramulla

Ushkar or Wushkar, according to Kalhana, is a corruption of the name Huvishka, the Kushan king from 2nd century AD. Due to the strategic trade-route position between Kashmir and north-western India, Ushkar became a flourishing trade town. King Lalitaditya built a shrine of Vishnu named Muktasvamin and also built a large *vihara* with a stupa at Ushkar. Kalhana mentioned in his historical chronicle that King Lalitaditya had built this in the 8th century. Famous Chinese pilgrim Hiuen Tsang, who had visited Kashmir in 631 AD, had entered the valley through the Baramulla passage and had stayed at one of the monasteries in this complex. The style of the shrine is similar to the one built at Parihaspura.

The lowest courses of its base are in position. Some years back during an excavation, an interesting revelation was unearthed. The shrine it seemed had been constructed on top of an older structure of nearly the same type, stones of which are built *in sui*. This old structure may have belonged to the Kushan times and is strengthened by the discovery of 11 terracotta heads. Head of a Boddhisattva, shaggy beard and knitted eyebrows of a Brahmic ascetic, a beautiful rounded face of *upasika* or a female devotee, and the head of a contemplative, dreamy-eyed young monk are some of the items that were discovered at the site. These are now preserved in the museum in Srinagar.

To the north of the stupa lie large block stones with inscriptions of *he-sh-ka-the*, written in Sharada script (the original script of Kashmir) on the hard surface, hinting at the colloquial name.

Another feature worth a mention is the boundary compact wall built out of extremely small chips of stone in mud. The base of the wall is extraordinarily thick and serves as the base for the length of cells which run along the entire length of the wall. The upper portion is utilized as their back wall. The foundation of the wall is pierced at intervals with openings for the drain. The entrance must have been from the east which is opposite to the stairs of the stupa. The other objects of interest are two erected Shiva-lingas.

Another nearby town now popular by the name of Baramulla, was originally called Varahamula. It got its name after the boar incarnation of Vishnu. The temple of Adi-Varaha or 'primeval boar' is said to have been a splendid creation of Kashmir but only a few architectural remains can be traced around. The only striking object left is a large human-faced Shiva-linga. Unfortunately, this temple was destroyed by Sikandar Butshikan.

II-43
Uri-Nowshera

On the highway between Uri and Nowshera, hidden behind an ambush of dried trees and shrubs are the ruins of an ancient temple, probably built in the 5th century. A part of the structure is still standing except that some of it has been plundered and wretched to demolition by invaders and later by the unrest in the valley. The four columns of the cella are visible, but the roof is missing. The carving on the cornice, frieze, and capital are faintly visible. Even in the thick of the ingrown trees and vegetation, steps leading to the sanctum along with the side railings are visible. General Cunningham tells it to be a Hindu temple with the image of Durga.

II-44
Utpal

It is believed that King Utpala, father of King Avantivarman had built this temple. This temple is dedicated to Lord Vishnu. *Rajatarangini* mentions that a city by the name of Utpalpura was established after the father's name.

The courtyard is square in shape and is 70 feet in size. An unornamented wall surrounds the complex and has a small opening on the east side. Ruins of once a porch, chamber, and cell can be seen now. A Vishnu idol in black stone was the main deity of the complex. The temple is now without a roof and was destroyed by Sikandar Butshikan.

II-45
Vichar *nag*

This was the seat of discussion of *panchangs, mahurats,* ceremonies, and religious contemplations. Legendary Shri Bhat, the architect of wisdom and the person who transformed Sultan Zainubidin 'Badshah', hailed from this area. Another learned man Pt. Vasudev, who had designed the 'almanac', which is still in use amongst the Kashmiri Pandit community, hailed from Vichar *nag*. It is located in Noushera, which is in the outskirts of Srinagar. It gained popularity because of these learned men, the two Shiva temples and a *nag*. The spring is approximately 430 feet in length and 35 feet in breadth. On the west and south sides of the spring, large devri stones have been used for the construction of the stairs. There is no access from the north and the east side. A boundary wall made of stones and images of Goddesses is constructed around the spring. In the middle of the spring a Shiva-linga rests on a cylinder. Water runs through small outlets and fills the spring before it reaches the famous Anchar Lake. The spring houses a variety of fish and the water has medicinal effects. It turns ice cold in summer and warm in winter. Like the Tulmul *nag* (mentioned later in the book) in Ganderbal, even the colour of the spring foretells good or bad news.

To the east of Vichar *nag* is the ancient Awanta Bhawan, constructed by Queen Amrita Prabha, wife of King Meghawahans. Kalhana has mentioned about Vichar *nag* in his epic book, stating that it was surrounded by willow trees and the Kashimir Pandits living in and around the temple lead a very simple and religious life.

Unfortunately, the ancient place of deliberation and a place where the Buddhist and Hindu councils were held, is in a despondent state today. The holy spring is filled with moss and plastic trash floats on the surface. Once a pious place, now there is filth all around.

II-46

Vishnu Ranaswamin

To the southwest of Vichar *nag* is Vishnu Ranaswamin, a fairly well-maintained shrine. Owning to its conversion to a *ziarat*, it is relatively well-preserved. There is an octagonal cella, and the high basement and high walls are well-preserved. Kalhana mentioned that this temple was found by King Ranaditya. He further adds that this temple must have been of considerable importance in Kashmir. Poet and historian, Mankah refers to this as an object of his father's devotion and historian Jonaraja in his comments in his version of *Rajatarangini* mentions that Vishnu Ranaswamin was one of the chief shrines of Pravarapura (the old name of Srinagar).

II-47

Vikrameshwara

In the north of Vichar *nag* is the temple of Vikrameshvara, built by King Vikramaditya (523–65 AD). The temple is in ruins now and some parts of the temple can be seen used in the construction of a school and a mosque.

II-48

Wular Lake

The ancient name for Wular Lake was Mahapadmasaras, taken from the name of the great serpent deity. There is folklore about the serpent deity who had cursed the lake and since then it is believed to be a deep lake with high and turbulent waves. Probably that's why the lake has derived its modern name from *ullola,* the Sanskrit name for 'high leaping waves'.

The popular lake of Srinagar city boasts of an island too, but unfortunately on this island the remains of an ancient temple are visible. A large assortment of fluted columns, stones from pilasters, jambs, etc. is scattered around the site. The structure was built of large blocks of limestone which are similar to the ones used in medieval Kashmir for temple building. The main external decorative feature is a double row of trefoil niches which are flanked by beautiful fluted columns surmounted by ribbed capitals. The lower row of niches stands on a twisted ovolo course and is surmounted by a filleted torus. The corner pilasters have square filleted capitals. The two flank walls of the porch have survived. The interior was paved with large stone flags. The floor was on a level with the filleted torus outside. These remains tend to prove that there was once a Hindu temple here.

This discovery is further strengthened by the presence of a big Shiva-linga, which can be been spotted on the eastern side of the island.

There is another structure on the island that also has material used from an ancient temple. It is a small domed chamber measuring 15.7 square feet. It is a sample of brick masonry and the string courses on top of the wall consist of projected wooden beams. Externally the walls are decorated with shallow arched recess, which were originally covered with plaster, and glazed tiles. These tiles have left a square impression on the back of the plaster, wherever it is visible. Even the entire chamber is coated with painted plaster. The debris of this structure can be spotted lying on the ground.

This small island is also popular by the name Suna Lank. During the reign of Zain-ul-Abidin (1420–70 AD), the lake was believed to stretch to the extent of Sambalpur, the present-day Sumbal. The stretched extent exposed the boats to sudden gales of winds and sometimes even loss of life. To prevent such accidents, the king created this islet as a landing place and boats could be moored there in the storm. He called this place Lanka and Zaina Dab (a small wooden enclosed balcony). Historian Jonaraja writes that King Zaina was anxious to build a one of a kind monument on the islet.

II-49
Zewan

Ten kilometres to the southeast of Srinagar lies the village of Zewan, whose ancient name was Javana. Zewan was described to be a 'place of high rising monuments'. This monument does not exist anymore, however the ruins are still there. Only a pool is left at the place now. It is popular by the name of Taksnaka Naga (Lord of Snakes) and is visited by people en route to Hareshvara Temple. It is believed that saffron plantation had originated from this spring and that its cultivation had spread to the neighbourhood too. Modern researchers were able to locate this ancient place based on the details mentioned by Bilhana, a historian and a poet from Kashmir. Bilhana was born at Khunmoh (located 5 km towards the east of Zewan), described the spring as 'a pool filled with pure water sacred to Takshak, the Lord of Snakes'.

During Akbar's rule, the cultivators worshipped at the spring at the beginning of each spring season. Even now, the cultivators of saffron products, most of whom are Muslims, offer revered milk into the spring as a good omen. Kalhana mentions Zewan as a place of *tirtha*; Abu-i-Fazal has mentioned about the holy place in his works.

Part III

Ancient Temples (Existing till date)

Time had come to leave. To bid goodbye. To tell the just-wed loved wife that I will be back. And, come back to re-live the renewed vows of peace, love and happiness. Kabir was all set to leave Srinagar and board that flight to California, yet there was one last job. He yearned to visit the Ashtha Bhairavs, Shankaracharya, Tulmul and Haeri Parbat temples. They weren't part of his research work but he wished to pay his obeisance to these temples which are highly venerated by the entire Kashmiri Pandit community, located across the globe.

III-50

Shankaracharya Temple

Srinagar

Shankaracharya temple is situated at the summit of the hill, which in ancient times was called Gopadri and Jyeshtheswara. Located in the heart of Srinagar city, it is the most conspicuous monument and attracts the attention of any visitor to the city. The ancient temple is at the top of the hill located at a height of 1,000 feet from the ground. The location of the temple is excellent. Atop the summit, the stunning expanse of Dal Lake and Nehru Park can be seen.

III-50a: The octagonal temple structure on hill top.

After the steep trek uphill through 243 steps, the visitor is duly rewarded when he spots the temple built of extraordinary stones, the panoramic view of Srinagar, and the spectacle of the mountain summits at the far end.

The hill is named so after the apostle of spirituality, Adi Guru Shankaracharya, who had travelled from Travancore to Kashmir to revive the Hindu Sanatan Dharma. He visited Kashmir during the time of Saint Abhinavagupt (993–1015 AD). Adi Guru Shankaracharya was a Vedantist and visited Kashmir with the intent of advancing Vedantic knowledge. At that time, the natives were firm and strong believers in the greatness of Shiva-Shakti, while Adi Guru Shankaracharya had different thoughts on this belief. There is a popular legend about how Shankaracharya experienced a strange awakening from an unknown woman in Kashmir and how that transformed him. One day he was hungry and when he saw a milkwoman carrying milk, he signalled at her asking for some milk. The milkwoman replied, that he might have to come down the hilltop to take milk, to which Adi Guru said that he had no *Shakti* or energy to come down the hill. At this response, the milkwoman immediately retorted, "Since you do not believe in *Shakti*, how would you have any *Shakti*?" He was taken aback by this comment and what followed was a religious discourse between the woman and Adi Guru Shankaracharya for many days. Adi Guru reflected on the experience and was convinced that her words were true, and thereafter accepted the supremacy of Shiva-Shakti. He meditated on this hill for many years and therefore the hilltop is consecrated with his name.

Many of his famous poems and hymns were composed on this hilltop. Around the same time, he composed the famous hymn called 'Soundarya Lahiri' and was a proponent of Advait Vedanta and Shaivism.

Structure

There is no clear information to the exact date of construction, however, the hillock has been as old as the valley itself. King Gopaladitya who reigned in the 3rd century had given a structure to the temple top. It was later repaired by King Lalitaditya in the 8th century. King Zain-ul-Abidin repaired the roof after it had tumbled down due to an earthquake. Sheikh Ghulam, a Sikh Governor, repaired the dome with brick masonry during his reign. There were steps of sculptured stones, leading from the Shudashyar *ghat* at the Jhelum river right up to the top of the hill. Many years later with these stones, Nur Jahan the wife of Jahangir built the Pathar Masjid which is located in the city.

The temple can be reached through a long flight of steps enclosed by two side walls, which originally bore Persian inscriptions. The temple is built on an octagonal plinth. The plinth is surmounted by a low parapet wall which is 23 feet 6 inches long on each side, the indoor of which was originally beautified by 84 round-headed recesses. The shrine has a cell with a diameter of 13 inches approximately. Externally it is square with two projecting facets on each side. The surface is plain except for the salient and re-entering angles of the facets and is 8 feet 2 inches in size. The interior of the ceiling is covered with stone and wooden slabs, and they rest on two lintels of the same material, supported on four columns in the centre of the room. The southwest column bears two Persian inscriptions, by a man named Bhisti (his name is engraved there), and can be traced back to the reign of Mughal ruler Shah Jahan. The original ceiling is dome-shaped and is constructed out of kanjur (a kind of light and porous limestone). The absence of a trefoiled entrance to the sanctum, and the similar niche on the other three sides is remarkable.

To the north of the base is a low cell, entered through a plain and a circular-headed low doorway. The ceiling is flat and is built of plain stone slabs, which rest on remarkably long beams supported on two octagonal columns. Slightly lower down to the southeast of the temple is a tank measuring 10 feet 1 inch.

III-50b: The 243 steps that go up to the sanctum.

The Zaberwan range which is dotted with Mughal gardens along the lower slope touching the shore of the Dal Lake is visible in the backdrop of the hill temple. A panoramic view of the huddled Srinagar rooftops, Haeri Parbat, both parts of the *Lakut* Dal *Bud* Dal (Small Dal and Big Dal Lake), Pari Mahal, Mahadev peaks, Boulevard Road that runs around the Dal Lake from Dalgate to Nishat Bagh and ahead, and rows of houseboats on the shimmering Dal Lake can be clearly seen from the temple top.

In the vicinity is the Adi Guru Shankaracharya cave, the spot where he meditated. It is a 'must-visit' place because Adiguru is credited with changing and reviving Hinduism in India.

History

The original date of construction has been a source of controversy amongst all researchers and archaeologists.

Kalhana in *Rajatarangini* mentions that King Gopaladitya built a shrine of Jyeshtheswara on the Gopadri Hill peak, but it cannot be ascertained that the present-day temple is the same. The shrine may still occupy the same position, but the same cannot be said with certainty for the building around it. It was near this hill, that the village of Bhuksiravatika (now known as Buchwara) was habituated by Brahmins; they had earned the patronage of King Gopaladitya. The land that the king had given to the Brahmins came to be known as Gopa Agrahara and now this land base is popular by the name of Gupkar. The village area where these Brahmins lived is now popular by the name of Galgate or Dalgate.

General Cunningham and Lt. Cole suggest that the temple was built during the times of King Jaluka (220 BC), who was another son of Ashoka the Great, but this theory was rejected on grounds of its architecture and the lack of authentic data. Another scholar on the architectural history of Kashmir, J. Ferguson writes that the temple was built by a Hindu devotee during the times of Jahangir, but after the bigoted Aurangzeb took over the reign of Kashmir, the Hindu devotee left the construction halfway. He infers this from the incomplete staircase and the date inscribed on it as 1659 AD. Since then the temple has had an unfinished look and has remained a ruin. Many other researchers do not concur with antiquarian Ferguson's thoughts and state that "Ferguson's conclusions are based on arguments which appear to have a weak foundation". Scholar Bernier who accompanied Aurangzeb to Kashmir in 1665, writes about the existence of a temple with idols in it.

One of the reasons for misleading information has been the unpardonable offence of scratching the structure of the temple. On the pillar in the southwest of the temple, a comment says, "The idol was made by Haji Hushti, who was a *sahukar* in the year 54 of the Samvat era." At the foot of the temple there is another comment which reads, "He who raised this temple is Khwaja Rukn, son of Mir Jan..." Researchers claim that there was no Islam at that time, so there is no possibility of this kind of a name and even if it was so, a Muslim would not build a temple with Samvat era written on it. The Muslims in Kashmir were too few in the beginning to initiate an architecture of their own.

Archaeologist Sir John Marshall thinks that the temple belongs approximately to the same period as the rest of the temples in Kashmir.

His Highness the Maharaja of Mysore had visited this temple in the 1930s and had further adorned it by building five electric searchlights around it and one on the top. These lights illuminate the temple and make it conspicuous from a faraway distance on the ground.

Relevance

The Shankaracharya temple of Kashmir commands one of the finest spiritual experiences in the valley.

This temple is among the few left which can still see a queue of devotees thronging it.

Hindu devotees visit this temple during the new moon phase, especially on Shivratri. They pay their respect to this temple when they embark on the pilgrimage to the holy Amarnath cave. *Shravan Poornima* is another important day to offer prayers to Lord Shiva. On this day devotees visit the temple and pray and sing all night seeking Shiva's blessings. The Buddhists call this temple Pas-Pahar and the Muslims (who changed the Hindu names of all places in Kashmir during their long rule) call it Takht-i-Sulaiman.

Besides Adi Guru Shankaracharya, Acharya Vinobha Bhave and Sri Aurobindo also paid their obeisance to the temple site. VIPs, senior bureaucrats, and other important dignitaries are frequent visitors to the holy site.

The temple is managed by the Dharmarth Trust, which was established in 1846 by Maharaja Gulab Singh. This trust was set up with the sole aim of restoring and maintaining the temples of Kashmir. As part of this endeavour, care-taking priests of the respective temples were put on a pay roll and welfare programs were initiated for them. Currently, Dr Karan Singh, the scion of the royal family, is the sole chairperson and trustee.

III-51
Tulmul Temple
Ganderbal

This temple is built inside a spring and is 25 kilometres away from Srinagar. It gets its name after the village Tulmul, which is located in the town of Ganderbal. The shrine of Ragnya Devi or Goddess Kshir Bhavani abodes here and this temple is the most revered and popular place of pilgrimage for the Kashmiri Hindus. An annual *mela* takes place at this temple, and the crowd of devotees is as large as the pilgrims for the annual Amarnath Yatra.

III-51a: The temple located inside a holy *nag*.

Structure

The spring is situated in the centre of an island, around which a canal from the Sindh river makes a circuit.

During ancient times the main spring was surrounded by 360 springs, which are now in oblivion and are covered with land. Out of these only four are existing now; namely, Ashtha Rudhar is to the south, Tsandar *nag* is to the southeast, and Mach *nag*, Nagarad, and Gokin *nag* are to the east. On the northeast of this island is Ganeshbal, where Lord Ganesh is worshipped.

The main spring has a small structure in the centre. There is a little island in the middle of the tank, on which a small temple must have been built. Now a small marble temple has been built at this place, inside which RajRajeshwari Maha Ragnya is seated along with Bhuteshvara. The temple was built further by Dogra ruler Maharaja Pratap Singh, who was a majestic and religious ruler. The floor of the island around the spring, upon which devotees can sit and pray is covered with stones. The walls of the *nag* are made of stone. Many years later Maharaja Hari Singh built a temple platform above the marble temple by erecting four pillars around it for protection of the marble temple. Silver umbrellas and flags presented by the devotees and worshippers of the 18-armed Goddess are installed inside the temple. The columns and roof are made of marble and the summit has one big and four small *shikhars* at the four corners. The main spring has a heptagonal shape, with the northern and the southern sides longer than the western sides.

But before the main spring came into existence, the Goddess was worshipped at a spot called Devotwol *boen* (colloquial name for Chinar tree). This spot was near the Chinar tree, which still exists.

Originally a marshy land, water that was sourced from the Sindh river, which eventually joined the Vitasta river, is now only a spring. At the end of the complex is a row of dharamshalas and havanshalas, constructed for the convenience of the devotees. At the entrance of the temple a bathing area is constructed which receives its supply of water from the gushing Sindh river.

During ancient times, devotees had to walk over marshy lands to pay their obeisance to the Goddess. Sometimes they would travel in *doongas* (wooden houseboats), *shikaras* (boats), or wade through the swampy and marshy land to reach to the Goddess. Some devotees would be fortunate to reach the spot and for some, the pilgrimage would turn out to be fatal, and they would unfortunately lose their lives on the way to the shrine. Ocassionally the entire path to the shrine would be laid with reeds for the safe walk of the pedestrians, but this was not successful in the long run.

During the reign of Maharaja Ranbir Singh, a merchant named Shah Radha Krishan paved the edge of the spring with Baramulla stones and Dewan Narsingh Dayal got a dharamshala built on the north side of the temple.

There are other important sites just before the entrance, a *ziarat* of Mir Baba Haider and a *samadhi* of saint Shri Labhu Shah, who lived for 150 years.

History

The name Tulmul originates from the village of Tulamulya. Some of the lore also credit the name with the swampy and soft land. The surface of the land was light and the flowers and vegetation were thick on the surface, giving it the look of a floating garden. 'Tool' means cotton and

'Mulla' means worth in Sanskrit. Hence the name Tulmul, for a place that is soft like cotton.

III-50b: The main gate of the temple complex.

Since ancient times, worshippers offer milk, sugar, and rice to the Goddess by pouring them into the *nag*. Over the many years this accumulated on the top level of the spring. Therefore, in 1867 AD, a man named Diwan Narshing Dayal cleaned the spring. Coincidently, around the same time a virulent cholera epidemic followed and took the lives of many Kashmiris. The appearance of this epidemic was superstitiously connected to the wrath of the Goddess, having been aroused by the disturbance of the spring. Since then no one dared to touch the spring for fear of again incurring the displeasure of the Goddess. For the longest time, the spring never got cleaned and as result, the water was disappearing and only the silt was visible. This again caused a lot of anxiety among the Hindu devotees. However, Pandit Vidh Lal Dhar took the bold decision of cleaning the spring.

In the process of cleaning up, not only did an enormous amount of deposits come out but an ancient temple was also unearthed. Large sculptured white stone slabs, some of which were nine feet long and three feet broad, were discovered. And since then, the existing shrine is thronged by devotees. The entire shrine was repaired with money raised through public subscriptions. The marble slab that can be seen in the main sanctum was erected by the Dogra rulers.

The water in the spring has a curious phenomenon to it. It changes its colours to light yellow, milky white, faint rosy, light green, purple, and even black at times. These changes in colour are a reflection of the times in the valley. If peace is prevailing, then the colour is teal and green but if the social situation is turbulent then the colour changes to black or dark purple. In 1947, when the Pakistani raiders attacked Kashmir, the spring water changed its colour to black. Again in 1990, when the Kashmiri Pandits were threatened and forced to leave their homeland, the colour of the spring had turned to black. The Hindu devotees of the shrine attribute this marvel to the manifestation of the Goddess Ragnya.

Worship of 'Mother', which is identical to the form of *Shaktis*, has an integral role in the Tantric form of worship which was prevalent in ancient Kashmir. The Ragnya-Kavach or the psalm in praise of the Goddess is included in an ancient Sanskrit book called *Rudrayamala-Tantra*. This goes on to say that the pilgrimage is an ancient one.

Under the rule of King Jayapida (753–784 AD), the *purohit* community of Tulmul was strong and influential. The king confiscated the temple area, which made the entire *purohit* community furious. One of the priests named Ittila cursed King Jayapida for his impious deeds. At that time, a gold pole of the canopy fell on the king's head, which caused him serious injuries resulting in his death eventually.

The *Mahatmaya* of the shrine mentions that the Goddess was originally in Ceylon (present Sri Lanka) and was revered by the demon King Ravana in her *Tamasi* form (that is black form), hence in Ceylon the Goddess was designated by the name *Shyama*. Ravana worshipped the Goddess with all his devotion to gain power and glory and the Goddess was pleased with his sober-minded worship. Ravana's grandfather, Rishi Pulatsya was one of the revered *sapt-rishis,* who resided in the Kashmir valley in the pre-epic times. But over time his conscience was so much covered with *Tamoguna* that it could not be purified even by making any offerings to the Goddess. Ravana's ego and self-pride had turned him into a demon. Due to Ravana's misdeeds, the wrathful Goddess cursed the demon king. After Ravana's death in the hands of Lord Rama, Hanuman, the divine companion of Rama was instructed by the Goddess herself to be carried to Satisar (another name for Kashmir), hence Hanuman bought the idol of *Shyama* or Parvati to Kashmir. It is said that Hanuman even carried 360 cows from Ceylon to the Kashmir valley. Hanuman selected a spot in the north of the valley and installed the Goddess with all her satellites. En route to Tulmul, Goddess Ragnya stopped at many village spots like Raithan (derives its name from Raygnia Stahan), which is located in Budgam; at Manjgom, which is located a little far from Kulgam; at Pokhribal, which is near Haeri Parbat; at Kulvagishwari, which is in Kulgam, and many other places before she finally rested at the Tulmul spring. The origin of the worship of Ragnya started from this place.

The same has been mentioned in a section of *Bringhish Samhita*, which is in the last chapter and is titled 'Ragnya Pradurbhava'. However, there is no such mention in the *Ramayana* or the *Mahabharata*.

Kashmir is a land of legends and stories. There once was a pious Brahmin named Brahman Krishna Pandit, who had a vision in which an angel told him about the existence of a spring in the lap of the marshy land of Tulmul. Upon hearing this he asked how would he know which direction to go. It is believed that the angel guided him and directed him to embark on a boat at Shadipur (confluence of Sindh and Vitasta), and a serpent will usher him to the spring. The point when the serpent jumps into the spring is the point of the abode of the Goddess. The serpent it seems moved in odd rectangular directions and the Brahmin followed the serpent marking the visited areas with a long stick. Poles were since then pitched there with flags, indicating the spring area, which was the abode of the Goddess. Prayers were held by the Brahmin and other Hindus to show their gratitude to the Goddess. At the end of the puja, it is believed that a birch bark was seen floating on the spring. The Brahmin pulled it out and saw revered *shlokas* inscribed on it. Moved by the infinite presence of the Goddess, the Brahmin was inspired to compose a poem of as many stanzas as there were letters in the *shlokas*. He continued to visit and offer sugar, milk, and rice to the holy shrine on every eighth day of the bright lunar fortnight.

Abu-i-Fazal, Akbar's biographer, has also mentioned in *Ain-i-Akbari* about a huge marshy land in Srinagar which was revered by the Hindus of the valley.

Relevance

Under Islamic rule, this place of worship was not visited by the Hindus; they feared being recognized and forced into conversion. It was only about 350 years ago when a man named Krishna Pandit Tapilu (descendants of whom are in the profession of fortune-telling), discovered the temple and since then it has been visited by flocks of devotees.

The Dogra rulers especially Maharaja Pratap Singh was a strong devotee of the Goddess and was extremely God-fearing. On every visit to the holy temple, he would offer a large quantity of milk and pray for hours. Maharaja Pratap Singh was weary of European visitors who often visited the holy shrine with their shoes on and even fished in these holy waters. This was highly disrespectful and the Maharaja was anxious about their movement around the swampy Tulmul area. He, therefore, issued a government decree putting a check on European visitors to the shrine.

The Tulmul temple Goddess has her mystic *Shri Chakras* too. Her *Shri Chakras* consist of sevens parts, one enclosed within another. They embody the Mother Goddess with her Shaktis. Sometimes bubbles rising out of water in the spring, form three lines of these *Shri Chakras*. These lines are the entry points or the *dwars* of the mystic *Shri Chakras*.

Zeath Ashtami (eighth day of the waxing moon fortnight) is the most auspicious day of the year and it is obligatory for Kashmiri Pandits to pay their obeisance to the Goddess on this day. So every month, boats, tongas, bullock-carts, and later in modern times buses would be loaded with devotees desiring to pray to the Goddess. *Hur Ashtami* (this day falls a few days prior to Maha Shivratri and the complete household is cleaned and prepped for the big day) is another equally important day for people to pay a visit to this temple.

Many seers and saints spent their period of penance around the spring of Maa Kheer Bhawani. And most popular have been the visits of Swami Vivekananda, Swami Ramteerth, and Adi GuruShankaracharya. Swami Vivekananda visited Tulmul shrine in 1894 and mentioned his experiences in the book *Talks with Swami Vivekananda*.

Quoting from the book, "Then Swamiji said, on the way back, he returned to Srinagar by the common route by which the pilgrims return. A few days after returning to Srinagar he went to visit Kshir Bhavani Devi. He stayed there for seven days and worshipped the Devi and made Homa to Her with offerings of Kshir (condensed milk). Every day he used to worship the Devi with Kshir as an offering. One day, while worshipping the thought arose in Swamiji's mind: *Mother Bhavani has been manifesting Her Presence here for untold years. The Mohammedans came and destroyed Her temple, yet the people of the place did nothing to protect Her. Alas, if I were then living, I could never have borne it silently*. When thinking in this strain, his mind was much oppressed with sorrow, and anguish, he distinctly heard the voice of the Mother saying: *It was according to My desire that the Mohammedans destroyed the temple. It is My desire that I should live in a dilapidated temple, otherwise, can I not immediately erect a seven-storied temple of gold here if I like? What can you do? Shall I protect you or shall you protect me?* Swamiji said: *Since hearing that Divine Voice, I cherish no more plans. The idea of building Maths etc. I have given up; as Mother wills, so it will be.*

Swami's disciple was speechless with wonder and began to think. 'Did he not one day tell me that whatever we saw and heard was but the echo of the *Atma* within me, that there was nothing outside?' The disciple fearlessly spoke out to the Swami, 'Sir, you used to say that Divine Voices are the echo of our inward thoughts and feelings.' Swamiji gravely said: *Whether it be internal or external, if you actually hear with your ears such a disembodied voice, as I have done, can you deny it and call it false? Divine Voices are actually heard, just as you and I are talking."*

This reproduction of the extract from the book goes on to say the influence the visit had on Swami Vivekananda.

Bakshi Ghulam Mohammad, the popular Prime Minister of the state, would visit this temple on *Zyetha Ashtami* day when it would be overcrowded with pilgrims from across the valley. Families would stay back for days together in the dharmshala, partly as a trip and partly for prayers, fasting, or muttering scriptures in groups. Hindu families in individual capacities and in groups would perform *havan* (the ritual of giving offerings to the Fire God to mark auspicious occasions like birth, marriage, etc.) here. Some families would even solemnize the holy thread ceremony of their child, which is considered to be a pious act. The temple premises had a circular shopping arcade meant for the sale of *luchees* (big size fried bread), fried lotus stems, and *halva,* which was later taken as *prashad* by the pilgrims on the concluding day. The temple was directly under Dharmarth Trust run by the Dogra clan and at present time too continues to be led by the scions of the Dogra family. After the treaty of Amritsar in 1846, under the rule of Gulab Singh many new constructions and renovation work was taken up to restore the ill-fated temples.

Even after the exodus, Tulmul continues to be a shrine of extreme reverence and devotion for Kashmir Pandits across the globe.

III-52

Haeri Parbat

Srinagar

श्री शारिका पातुनः
सर्व सिद्धि दायिनी,
महा भय नाशिनी,
ग्रह पीडा निवारिणि।

Dominant and all-powerful Sanskrit *shlok* written in red ink at the entrance of the Haeri Parbat temple complex is an imposing first impression of the holy place. The most divine place, which has been revered by the Kashmiri Pandits with the utmost humble attitude since times immemorial, is the nerve centre of their spiritual journey.

In the late 16th century, Mughal emperor Akbar fortified the hillock as part of his plan to change the capital city to the site of modern-day Srinagar. The pivot location of the hill was luring enough for Akbar, but unfortunately, he could not accomplish the task. It was in the early 19th century that the Governor of the Durrani Empire (from Afghanistan), built the current fort.

The fort is located on the west side of the famous Dal Lake and can be entered from two sides—via the Kathi Darwaza gate of Rainawari and the Sangin Darwaza gate of Hawal. The place has been of prominence for a gurudwara, a temple, and a shrine.

Structure

The fort is at the summit of the hillock. The structure is built in accordance with Vastushastra and it is located at the centre of the city, which marks the centre of the *Shri Chakra* as well. During the early times, the valley was called Nagar-Nagar, and the name of the city Srinagar came from the amalgamation of *Shri Chakra* and Nagar-Nagar.

III-52a: The stairs that lead to the holy temple.

The ramparts which are largely in ruins are on a circumference of approximately 3 kilometres. The Kathi Darwaza side has Akbar's inscriptions written on it, and it can be deduced that this must have been the primary entrance to the fort. It is a simple structure, comprising a domed chamber in the middle with two side-recess. The only outside decorations are the rectangular and arched panels and two beautiful medallions, in high relief on the spandrel of the arch.

On the Gojwara side within the outer wall there is an old structure which was known as the King Pravarsena's palace. It was King Pravarsena who had laid the foundation of Srinagar city. Inside the palace there was a temple built for the king, but the temple does not exist anymore. Folklores say that at the time of the death of King Pravarsena, he ejected from the roof of his palace and never came back.

The Sangin Darwaza or the stone gate is more ornate than the Kathi Darwaza. The exterior is decorated with two corbelled windows, and there are two staircases, one on each side, that give access to the roof.

According to local tradition, the work on the ramparts was started as relief work, to alleviate the distress of the people during the famine. According to historian Suka, the Mughal emperor upon hearing the hardships inflicted upon the citizens by the troops, who for want of accommodation had quartered upon them, had a cantonment built on the slopes of Haeri Parbat hill. French traveller Bernier, many centuries later called it "an isolated hill, with handsome houses on the declivity, each having a garden".

However, the formation and the existence of the hillock dates back to pre-historic times and has high reverence among the Kashmiri Pandits.

History

The hill of Haeri Parbat, crowed by the fort is visible from every corner of Srinagar. *Sarikaparvata* (hill of Sarika), or Sharika Peeth has been a place of great sanctity for Hindus of the valley. Legend, corroborated with modern science, apprises that during pre-historic times, the valley was a lake. In this lake lived a demon called Jalobhava who had created havoc among the valley dwellers. *Sarikamahatmaya* informs us how the celestial powers fought and waged an unsuccessful war against the water demon, who was at a disadvantage on the land and therefore fought all the battles from beneath the water. Finally, the Gods implored Mother Sati, controller of the titanic forces of nature. Taking the form of a Sarika bird (mynah), she took a pebble in her beak and dropped it at the spot in the lake where she knew that the demon would be lying. The pebble swelled to an enormous size and crushed the demon inside the water. To this day that gigantic stone is called Haeri Parbat.

A depression outside the Sangin Darwaza, points out to the place wherefrom the panting breath of Jalobhava created a cavity, because he was getting crushed under the weight of the heavy boulder. The legend adds that the Gods, in grateful memory of the deliverance of the killing of the demon, made Haeri Parbat their abode. This adds to the fact that every stone, big or small on the hillock is considered to be an abode of the 33 *Koti* (symbolic for levels) Gods and Goddesses which compromise the Hindu pantheon.

III-52b: Inside of the main temple.

Relevance

Trupursundari, with 18 arms, is the presiding deity of Srinagar city. She resides at Haeri Parbat in the form of the mystic *Shri Chakra* or the *Maha Yantra*. This *Shri Chakra* or *Mandala* is self-engraved on the *Shila* (summit of the hill-lock in a stone form) and therefore gets the name of Chakreshwari or Chakreshwar. On a full moon night, the white soft light shines on the impression of *Shri Chakra* on the *Shila* and it reflects surreal rays into the surroundings.

The *Maha-Yantra* is a distinct form consisting of circles, nine triangles, and lotus petals. The four triangles facing upwards represent *Shiva* and the five triangles facing downwards represent *Shakti*, and respectively are called *Shiva Kanthas* and *Shiva Yuktis*. The intersecting of these triangles represents creation, protection, and absorption of the universe by the divine force called 'Sudha-Shakti'. *Shri Chakra* is charged with supreme occult energy. At the centre is the *Bindu*, which is independent of *Shiv Kanthas* and *Shiv Yuktis* and thus symbolizes the union of Shiva and Shakti. This Bindu is the mysterious matrix of the *Maha-Yantra*.

These upward and downward-facing triangles intersect to form 43 big and small triangles. All of them are enclosed within the innermost circle, on which is drawn a lotus with eight petals and is called 'Ashtha-Dal'. This represents the mystical seed of creation. Outside this circle is another circle with 16 lotus petals representing the 16 phases of the moon. This entire set of triangles and lotus petals is further enclosed inside a triple concentric circle called 'Trimekhla'. This mystical *Shri Chakra* is placed inside a square with triple parallel lines, having four openings in the four cardinal directions.

The wheel of the universe is identified with the *Shri Chakra* or *Maha Yantra*.

If one looks attentively at the *Shri Chakra* formation, the geometrical design of the *Shri Chakra* is visible on the rock smeared in vermillion. During bright sunny days, the lines of the triangles and their apex in the crowded form are more vivid to the eye. The smeared vermillion and purified ghee on the *shila* surface, which has accumulated over so many centuries, can be clearly seen in the grooves of the *Shri Chakra*, hence giving a more astounding impact of the *Shri Chakra*. But during summer, the ghee melts away and the paste becomes loose and trickles down the surface. And the geometrical design again stands out clearly to the naked eyes.

In an expression of complete renunciation before Goddess Sharika, devotees would circumambulate the temple for straight 40 days. Neither the heat of the summers nor the death defying winters could dampen their devotion. During the peaceful co-existence times, devotees would spend all weekends, especially Saturdays reciting Lalitasahastranam, Panchatavi, and other *bhajans* in praise of Chakreshwari. On auspicious days like *Haerath* (Shiv-ratri), *Navreh* (New Year), *Shiv-chaturdeshi, Krishan Janamasthami*, there would be a large crowd of devotees trailing around the Haeri Parbat for circumambulation. Saturdays and Sundays were also the days when devotees would offer yellow rice along with cooked vegetables as an offering to the Goddess. Sacrificial offerings were also common at the temple, and the food was later offered to the kites, hovering over the top. The temple offered sustenance to a number of purohit families, who had housed at the foot of the Haeri Parbat hillock in the Devi-*angan* location. Each purohit family had kept a separate Kosak for those morning visitors who used to take the outer trail for circumambulation along the foothill path, because they did not have time to go up to Chakreshwar temple. Indira Gandhi, former Indian PM, had visited Chakreshwar, and M.L. Fotedar (Senior leader and Minister in the National Congress Party) had also visisted the temple complex.

Chakreshwar had a regular elected body with office-bearers who were taking care of the temple and its property at the foot of the hill. Every year a *hawan* was performed here by the committee and every common Kashmiri would also solemnize *hawan* if their wishes were accomplished.

The complex has many temples in the vicinity.

MahaGanesh, also popular as Ganeshbal, located on the eastern side has been there since times immemorial. In his version of *Rajatarangini,* historian Jonaraja, and educationist Tyndale Biscoe mention that when Pravarsena II established the new city of Pravarapura (present-day Srinagar), Ganesha who sat on the hilltop turned his head towards Pravarapura to bless the new city.

Sapt-Rishi, symbolized by a tree, is a shrine where devotees pay obeisance to the *sapt-rishis* to whom Kashmiri Pandits trace their genealogy.

Maha-Kali is the *asthapana,* devotees pay their respect to.

Devi-angan is a compound that is dotted with many temples, but in recent times, many houses have mushroomed in this area.

Chakreshwar is at an elevation of 200 feet above ground level and is the abode of Mata Sharika. The shrine is known for the mystical *Shri Chakra* and can be reached after taking a flight of 100 steps.

Haeri Asthapana is located on the western side of the hillock. It is dedicated to Mata Sharika and has been a spot for meditation for seers and saints for ages.

Mahalakshmi temple is opposite the shrine of Haeri Asthapana. Alongside beautiful gardens, this compound houses Amar Koul, Mahalakshmi, and Sita Ram temples.

Hanuman temple is the last point devotees stop at after circumambulation of the entire temple complex of Haeri Parbat. It is next to Kathi Darwaza.

Haeri Parbat complex is the fountainhead of the cultural civilization of Kashmir valley. Many saints, yogis, seers, and holy scholars have visited this Shakti Peeth since pre-historic times, and their energies and vibrations can still be felt in the temple compound. Even according to Vastushastra, this complex is located in the centre of Srinagar city. Therefore, it is believed that any devotee who visits Chakreshwar is believed to have obtained all his worldly wisdom and well-being.

Sahitya Akademi awardee, artist Ghulam Rasool Santosh had mentioned Haeri Parbat to be older than the Indian civilization. As per him, the complex houses the entire pantheon of Hindu Gods and Goddesses. Many mystic saints of Kashmir were believed to have spent their periods of penance at this temple to fulfil their spiritual or divine quests. It was considered to be a *Seedht Peeth* meaning one would get spiritual enlightenment if one undergoes rigorous penance and prayers at Haeri Parbat because of its rich divine vibration.

Part IV

The Ashtha Bhairavs

IV-53

Ashtha Bhairav

Bhairav is a widely worshipped form of Shiva. He is the ferocious manifestation of Shiva and literally means, 'one with the frightening cry or the terrible one'. In Vedantic tradition, Bhairavs are part of the Shiva's army (also referred to as *Shivaganas* or *Bhutaganas*), and are therefore the guardians. In the Shaivite tradition, Bhairavs have been elevated to the status of Shiva Himself, Who destroys the weakness of the lower self. They are demigods, with their own unique characteristics, and are propitiated along with other Gods at all important religious ceremonies. Bhairavs represent the five elements of water, air, earth, fire and space.

Etymologically, Bhairav represents a combination of three aspects of Lord Shiva—*Bha,* which comes from *Bharena,* and means maintaining the Universe; *Ra,* which comes from *Revana,* and means withdrawal of Universe; and lastly *Va,* which comes from *Vatmana,* and means emitting or letting go of Universe. Therefore, Bhairav represents the three aspects of Shiva, which are *Srishti, Stehti* and *Samhara* which mean manifestation, maintenance and withdrawal respectively.

In the 5th century, King Pravarsena II designed and built the city of Srinagar. The city was planned to have important entry points to the city. There were designated eight gates for the eight *Bhairavs* and ten *Dikpalas*. These eight *Bhiaravs* had attained spiritual emancipation and had become Shiva like in character. Each of these *Bhairavs* are credited with the creation of further seven Bhairavs. Likewise, the *Dikpalas* were not only the guardian of the nine cardinal directions but also the guardian of the sacred place of worship. Some also view Bhairav as a form of Khetrepala, also revered as the protecting and the sheltering deity.

Anandeshwar Bhairav is the presiding Bhairav of the entire Srinagar city and the rest are the guardians of the different localities of Srinagar city. Each Bhairav is the guardian of a particular area and protects the residents from any adversity. In most of these Bhairav temples, a certain date on the waning moon fortnight of the lunar calendar was a day of celebration and festivity.

Listed below are the original places where the eight Bhairav temples were constructed by King Pravarsena II, but unfortunately they have been decimated and even their ruins are not traceable now. Their land has been encroached upon and many modern structures have been built on top of them. They are beyond recognition for people who would have seen them in their prime during the good old days.

IV-53a

Anandeshwar Bhairav

This Bhairav temple is located at Maisuma, a locality in the uptown area of Srinagar. It is near the Dashnami Akhada in Amira Kadak area. He is the protector of Sathu, Amira Kadal and Ganpatyar areas of Srinagar city.

The Jayanti celebration of Anandeshwar Bhairav falls on *Posh Krishna Paksh Dashmi*, which in the local parlance is known as *Poh Ghatapach Dahum*. Anandeshwar Bhairav is the superior most amongst all Bhairavs of Srinagar city and the entire of Kashmir *mandal*.

IV-53b

Bahukhateshwar Bhairav

This Bhairav's abode is located at the confluence of Vitasta and Dudh Ganga rivers. This place is spotted in the Chattbal area. Majestic willow and chinar trees which are spread over an area of 2 kanal, add an aesthetic charm to the temple complex.

IV-53c

Hatkeshwar Bhairav

This temple is located at Malakhah, next to the Kathi Darwaza area near Haeri Parbat. On return from Chakreshwar, devotees would pay their obeisance at the temple. However, at the moment there is no trace of this Bhairav temple.

IV-53d

Mangaleshwar Bhairav

The abode for this Bhairav is inside a mulberry tree which is located at a temple at Namchibal at the Fateh

Kadal area of Srinagar city. The temple is located on an island and a boat is ferried by the devotee to visit this Bhairav. The entire complex is on an area of 1.5 kanal of land. A particular date in the new moon fortnight on the lunar calendar is celebrated as the birthday of Mangaleshwar Bhairav.

IV-53e
Puranaza Bhairav

This Bhairav temple is located at Sazigaripora area in Srinagar. He is the protector of Haeri Parbat, Safa Kadal and Ali Kadal localities of Srinagar city. Annual prayers are held during the waning moon fortnight of the lunar calendar.

IV-53f
Sheetalnath Bhairav

This temple is located inside the famous Sheetal Nath complex. Besides the temple, the complex is famous for the lectures addressed by Indira Gandhi, Vir Savarkar, Jawahar Lal Nehru. The temple which is spread over 6 kanal of land houses the Hindu High School as well. Prior to the exodus of the Kashmiri Pandits from their homeland, *Basant Panchami* was the most celebrated festival in this temple complex. After a gap of 31 years, a group of Kashmiri Hindus performed the festival of *Basant Panchami* here in 2021.

IV-53g
Tushkraza Bhairav

The temple for this Bhairav is located in the Narsinghgarh locality near Karan Nagar area. This Bhairav is the protector of Karafolli Mohalla, Shalla Kadal, Zaindar Mohalla, Habba Kadal, Karan Nagar, Narsinghgarh, Bal Garden, and Kani Kadal. During the good old times, a certain date during the waning moon fortnight on the lunar calendar was the annual festival of celebration at the temple of Bhairav.

IV-53h
Vitalraza Bhairav

There are two Vitalraza Bhairav temples in the Rainawari area of Srinagar. The first Bhairav, which is also popular by the name of Boed Bhairav (Big Bhairav) resides inside a mulberry tree, which is located in an area of about 3 kanal of land. The second Bhairav temple also popular as *Lakut* Bhairav (Small Bhairav) is located in the Motiyar locality of Rainawari. This temple complex has a Shiva and a Devi temple. The Devi idol is in black stone and was ferried from South India by Kanna Swamiji who was the presiding Swamiji of the temple. After the exodus of Kashmiri Pandits from the valley in 1990, the mulberry tree was cut down by the perpetrators and is presently only a stub inside the temple complex.

Epilogue

Six months. Six golden months. The memory of each day, each event, and each moment were fresh like yesterday in Kabir's mind.

Kabir was seated in the middle row. Nadira was seated in the front row. His other gang of friends was scheduled on some other day for their 'hooding ceremony'. None of his friends was around to notice his nervousness. No one was around to tap on his oscillating feet. The young doctoral graduate was in a predicament. And the cause for this dilemma was the accidental accomplishment of all his dreams at the same time. Here he was in the Zellerbach Hall, waiting for the professor to call out his name and confer the doctoral degree upon him, and yet his mind was in a mess. By this evening, he had to give his consent for the job role of an Associate Professor at the University of California.

A couple of months ago when he took the farewell flight from Srinagar to New Delhi, he carried a burden. The burden of a silent promise he had made to himself. Kabir's temple research result had left him hungry for more. He had already got a couple of faculty offers from various leading universities in India. They were keen on hiring him. Kabir had sent a positive response to Banaras Hindu University, where he was offered the role of an Assistant Professor in the Centre for Kashmir Studies. They accommodated and were willing to wait for Kabir to receive his doctoral degree.

On the day of his departure, at the waiting lounge of Srinagar airport, Shakeel advised, "You are lucky to get this opportunity. But don't take it in the heat of the moment. Think. Mull over it. We often jump into the first available option life throws at us and then repent later. You have lived 15 years of your life outside of India. It won't be a cakewalk for you here. Life is different here. The only time you should think about the BHU (Banaras Hindu University) offer is when you are back in your dorm at the University. If you still miss being in Kashmir, then Kabir you would know for sure where your heart is heading."

The last few months had not been easy for Kabir. Reading, editing, re-editing, interviewing, long calls, meetings with his heads of department, and a thousand such other drills before walking up on the stage for the doctorate; it had been a laborious journey. He had missed so many social and cultural events on and off campus. The Asian community and the popular 'Indian Food Folks', had hosted a string of gastronomic events across the Bay Area, but Kabir, who was otherwise always the first one to arrive, attended none this time.

Those months in Kashmir had turned him into a different man. He didn't wish to celebrate India and her richness like this. On a borrowed land, at a borrowed time—this jingoism wasn't his idea of Nation love. Celebrating the culture, food, art, clothes, and many more things about India is one thing. But a more decisive resolve was required to ensure that each Indian is contributing and weaving a story worth narrating to the next generation. He pondered and thought that his story cannot be romanticized unless there is an emotion of despair, and separation in it. He was affirmative that by sitting in the posh staff room of the University of California, he wouldn't be able to narrate that story. He knew it wasn't about any sort of activism, but it was about owning the 'glorious past', and displaying that feeling of the 'glorious past' with pride.

A few days before the event, Kabir had returned the borrowed books, cleared the accounts with the laundry, handed over the dorm keys, and sorted all the aligned jobs. He was convinced about the plan he had created for his future, and his movements on campus were a clear indicator for outsiders. Yet, in his heart, a tinge of uncertainty lingered. The evening before the ceremony, his father called up to congratulate him on the big day ahead. Although Kabir's father was keen on attending his felicitation, his farm work kept him busy, and therefore he conveyed his wishes over a WhatsApp call. Like all concerned parents, Kabir's father was crisp in sharing his life experiences and giving his parental advice. Otherwise a man with a baritone voice, that day his voice was meek.

It was his last day of hope; for Kabir to return to India. His father had been living alone on that farm after Kabir's mother had passed away. It had been more than 20 years since he chose to relive his farmland dream in the hillocks of Shimla. Kabir was born in this small hamlet and he had been away from Shimla since the age of 15. Kabir's ancestors had fled the valley because of the atrocities by the Afghan invaders on Kashmiri Hindus during the 17th century. They along with many other families had finally settled in various parts of the plains of India.

"Sorry, I wasn't able to come. This is the harvest season. I have to reap the fruits of the seed I had sowed. It is as ethereal as I say, Kabir, even you would be harvesting the fruits of your hard work. You have worked hard to earn this degree and the most prestigious job of a faculty at your alma mater. Best wishes always... Well, now some farm update, I have finally hired two more people to manage the store and the warehouse. With each passing day, arthritis is challenging my daily routines. Hopefully, they should be able to nurture the farm the way, your mother and I had desired. Your grandmother must be proud of you today. She always wanted to visit the temples, shrines, villages, lanes, valleys, *nags*, and pilgrimages, you were researching on. Unfortunately, I wasn't able to take her to our native land. How I wish she was alive to see this. She would have circumambulated you!"

Kabir was silent, but his father had unconsciously cleared Kabir's clouded mind. His father had no clue about the mess Kabir was in. The unsettlement of so many months was at its pinnacle that day.

After a wait of one hour, his name was called out. Kabir was nervous, but just enough for an occasion like this. The cloak, cap, degree citation, and all the academia regalia were conferred upon him. His acceptance speech was a blitz of emotions—a heady mix of missing the opportunities of working in a cosmopolitan world, and of the excitement of unveiling the truth about the land of his ancestors.

"I always thought that I was the modern nomad. A man who moved places, searching for new-age opportunities, growth, learning, and intellectual development. I am grateful to the

Almighty that I could afford these luxuries and hobnob with the academicians of the world. But my field research in Kashmir has awakened the real learner in me. How could I call myself a nomad when I do not know the previous destination I come from? How could I claim to have a doctorate in philosophy when I have no insight into the glorious past I come from? I think those innumerable monuments, temples, and shrines in Anantnag, Pattan, Pulwama, Awantipora, Baramulla, Loduv, and many other towns, and villages were my places of calling. Those structures made of mammoth stones, and compounds that had been deserted for centuries had a story to tell. I had felt that their stories and miseries had been muffled by every ruling organization in the valley. They were bruised, betrayed, and abandoned by everyone in the valley. Somebody had to speak for them, talk about them and respect them because we Kashmiris are what we are because of our illustrious past.

Since my childhood days, I was told the stories of the valour of the Kings and Queens of Kashmir. Of those times when their reign was from the seas of Odisha to the extremes of Afghanistan, from the arid region of Ladakh to the plains of Kanauj and Magadha. My grandmother narrated these stories with so much emotion and passion. I would often see tears rolling down her plump cheeks. I was too naive and young to understand the cause of her grief. Years later, when I had to make a subject choice in my academic career, 'Ancient History and Architecture', chose me, rather than the other way. And today, as I stand here, equipped with enough awareness to earn a doctorate, yet I do not have enough wisdom to spread the strength of this past. I have to walk many more miles because I have now understood the meaning of those helpless tears. They were the crude remnants of loss and separation from her native land. My ancestors are the aborigines of this great land of Kashmir, which once upon a time boasted of Vijeshwara (now a sleepy town in the district of Anantnag), which was the fountainhead of knowledge. The mere gasp of the environs of Vijeshwara would turn an unschooled person into a scholar.

It's about time I pay back and honour my forbearers, who are a part of my personality today. They have laid the foundation for an entire civilization, an entire country, and an entire set of the human race. The history of this period in the Kashmir valley cannot be ignored and put under the carpet any longer. Those silent custodians of an ancient civilization have waited enough. The world needs to know and acknowledge the majestic past of my native land." Kabir left the hall amidst a roaring applause from his peers and the teachers.

A few weeks after joining BHU, Kabir went to Shimla to spend the weekend with his father. Ecstatic and joyous, Kabir's father welcomed him with wide arms of longing.

References

Books

Kheer Bhawani, by Samsar Chand Kaul.

Ancient Buildings in Kashmir, by Henry Hardy Cole.

Archaeological Remains in Kashmir, by Anand Koul Bamzai.

Beautiful Valleys of Kashmir and Ladakh, by Samsar Chand Kaul.

Places of Worship, by Chander M. Bhat.

Cultural Heritage of Kashmiri Pandits, edited by Dr. S.S. Toshkhani and Dr. K. Warikoo.

Ancient Monuments of Kashmir, by R.C. Kak.

The Valley of Kashmir, by Walter L. Lawrence.

A History of Kashmiri Pandits, by Justice J.L. Kilam, edited by Dr. Advaitavadini Kaul.

Kashmir—History and Archaeology through the Ages, by S.L. Shali.

Travels in Kashmir and Panjab, by B.C. Hugel.

Socio-Cultural and Religious Traditions of Kashmiri Pandits, by Piyaray Raina (Saddhak).

Rajatarangini I and *II,* by M.A. Stein.

Neelmatpuran I and *II,* by Ved Kumari.

Online/Papers/Articles/Books

https://searchkashmir.org/

http://ikashmir.net/

https://www.youtube.com/watch?v=zrt8da3fqRQ/bhairav vimarsh/

https://ignca.gov.in/PDF_data/Ancient_Temples_Kashmir.pdf
https://travelthehimalayas.com/
https://open.library.ubc.ca/media/stream/pdf/70440/1.0391987/2
https://archive.org/
https://www.dailyexcelsior.com
http://hindutemples-india.blogspot.com
https://kashmirblogs.wordpress.com
https://www.kalasamaymagazine.com/publication.html

Picture Credits

Aditya Raj Kaul
Chander M. Bhat
Ravinder Pandita
Sunil Raina Rajanaka
vmis.in
Vinayak Razdan

Photographs Index

Photo no.	Temple Name	Page No	Description
I-8a	Loduv	73	Main temple standing in the middle of a water body.
I-8b		77	Broken image of a divine figure lying outside.
I-9	Mamaleshwar	82	Temple with two fluted columns.
I-10a	Manasbal	82	Top of the partially submerged temple.
I-10b		85	Old picture of the temple surrounded by marshy land.
I-11a	Martand	88	The grand colonnade entrance of the temple.
I-11b		95	Old picture of people attending a festival in the temple complex.
I-12a	Naaranag	99	Dismantled structure of the main temple.
I-12b		106	The entire temple complex with many small structures.
I-13a	Narasthan	109	View from the entrance of the temple compound.
I-13b		113	The fragmented boundary walls of the temple.
I-14a	Pandrethan	114	The leaning temple structure submerged in water.

Photo no.	Temple Name	Page No	Description
III-50a	Shankaracharya	184	The octagonal temple structure on hill top.
III-50b		188	The 243 steps that go up to the sanctum.
III-51a	Tulmul	191	The temple located inside a holy *nag*.
III-51b		200	The main gate of the temple complex.
III-52a	Haeri Parbat	202	The stairs that lead to the holy temple.
III-52b			Inside of the main temple.

Acknowledgements

The phone call from Dipankar Mukherjee, Founder, and Director at Readomania Publishing, based in New Delhi led me into embarking on the most enriching experience. This book-writing experience filled me further with so much more love and pride for my homeland. Thank you, Dipankar.

A special thank you to Indrani Ganguly, who has been more than an editor to me. Her constructive and encouraging feedback makes her the most uncomplicated and easy editor to work with. She has a heart of gold.

I would like to express my heartfelt thank you to Dr K.N. Pandita for sharing his vast expertise on the subject. His insight has greatly enriched each chapter of this book.

I would like to extend my deepest gratitude to Dr K. Warikoo for his unwavering belief in the importance of the narrative. His valued feedback, suggestions and mentoring has shaped this book.

I wish to extend my deepest respect to my spiritual guide Mr Surendranath Kaul for his continued blessings throughout the process of book writing.

I would like to express my deep gratitude to Mr R.L. Shali for assisting in accessing the necessary resources.

I am immensely grateful to Dr Advaitavadini Kaul, who passionately guided me with the innumerable details, that underpins this book. She graciously shared her experiences, learnings and stories which form the heart of this book.

This book would not have been possible without the incredible support of Mr Chander M. Bhat. His tireless facilitation in guiding me with data, information and pictures has given a new depth to this book.

Thank you to Mr Anil Nakhasi for the map.

I would like to express immense love to my younger brother Aditya Raj Kaul for his unwavering encouragement and rock solid support. I appreciate how kind-heartedly and magnanimously he embraced my wishes and contributed to the creation of this book.

Avanti Sopory
Gurugram, 2023

About The Author

Kashmir being her first love; author and educator, Avanti wrote *Catching The Fading Ray,* which is a collection of folk tales from her native place. They are a reflection of the rich cultural reminiscence of the author's formative years at her birthplace.

In her last book titled *The Kashmir That Was,* Avanti brought forth the bygone times when Kashmir was romanticised. This book is a collection of flash back moments where the unseen, unheard, unimagined side of Kashmir converge to reveal a new facet of the erstwhile state, and it has been accepted very well by the readers.

Avanti has been a part of various anthologies titled, *Crossed and Knotted, Defiant Dreams, When They Spoke and The Readomania book of Mythology.* Her opinion pieces are published in Jammu-based *Daily Excelsior, Women's Web, Madras Courier,* and *Early Times.* She is a fellow at 'The Way of Writing with Natalie Goldberg'.

Writing to her is an unruffled world of her own, where her creations and people come to life.

Follow Avanti at:

Blog – undermynose.in

Facebook – htttps://www.facebook.com/avasopory

Instagram – @avkaul

X/Twitter – @ASopory

Readomania

Readomania exists to nurture, curate, and bring to you content you love. We are a publishing house that takes pride in encouraging talent, new or old, and provides a wonderful platform for awesome stories.

We make this possible in multiple ways.

The first as an independent publishing house. Readomania boasts of multiple imprints across various categories—fiction, nonfiction, children, to name a few. An eclectic mix of content for its readers, when you read a Readomania title, you enter a world that's yours, supported by unique and quality narratives.

The second, as an online publishing platform for writers—a place to share stories, poems, opinions, travelogues, a way to explore your creative talent. Available as premium, as well as free-to-read content across multiple genres, the reader is spoilt for choice.

Join us in this journey, as we explore, develop, and present stories to our readers and audiences. Welcome to the world of Readomania, get ready to craft stories that enrich lives.

You can visit us at: www.readomania.com